2/24

THE
BEST OF
BROCHURE
DESIGN 9

ROCKPORT

The Best of
BROCHURE DESIGN **9**

JASON GODFREY

BEVERLY MASSACHUSETTS

ROCKPORT PUBLISHERS

CONTENTS

First published in the United States of America by
Rockport Publishers, Inc., a member of
Quayside Publishing Group
100 Cummings Center
Suite 406-L
Beverly, MA 01915-6101
Telephone: (978) 282-9590
Fax: (978) 283-2742
www.rockpub.com

ISBN-13: 978-1-59253-282-7
ISBN-10: 1-59253-282-9

10 9 8 7 6 5 4 3 2

Design: Jason Godfrey at Godfrey Design
www.godfreydesign.co.uk

Printed in China

INTRODUCTION

DESIGNER >

CLIENT >

BRIEF >

RESEARCH >

IDEA >

PRESENTATION >

REVISIONS >

WRITING >

ART >

APPROVAL >

PRINTING >

BOX >

MAIL >

LAUNCH >

DISTRIBUTE >

PARTY >

SELL >

READ >

SHARE >

KEEP >

ENJOY >

RESPOND >

REPRINT >

CALL FOR ENTRIES >

SUBMISSIONS >

MORE SUBMISSIONS >

WORLD-WIDE SUBMISSIONS >

CATALOGING >

JUDGING >

ARRANGE >

PHOTOGRAPH >

LAYOUT >

PRINT >

SELL >

ENJOY >

MANY THANKS

JASON GODFREY

ANNUAL
REPORTS

SAS DESIGN
001, 016

SAGMEISTER INC.
002

SALTERBAXTER
003

ATELIER WORKS
004

CAHAN & ASSOCIATES
005, 009, 011, 019

HAT-TRICK DESIGN
006

THE CHASE
007

BILLY BLUE CREATIVE, PRECINCT
008

FROST DESIGN, SYDNEY
010

LIPPA PEARCE
012

NB:STUDIO
013, 020

IRIDIUM, A DESIGN AGENCY/ KOLEGRAM
014

BLUE RIVER
015

SONSOLES LLORENS S.L
017

DOPPIO DESIGN
018

PENTAGRAM DESIGN, SAN FRANCISCO
021

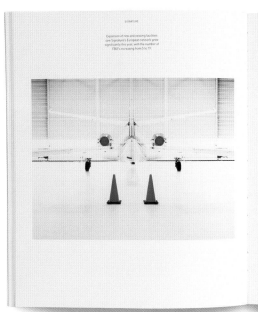

SAS DESIGN
BBA
Annual Report &
Accounts
001

Art Directors:
David Stocks,
Gilmar Wendt
Designer:
Mike Hall
Client:
BBA
Software:
QuarkXPress
Paper|Materials:
Medley Pure, Ikonosilk

COLUMBIA UNIVERSITY
GRADUATE SCHOOL OF ARCHITECTURE
PLANNING AND PRESERVATION
ABSTRACT 03/04

ADVANCED ARCHITECTURE STUDIO
STUDIO 5

SAGMEISTER INC.
Columbia University Annual Publication
002

Art Directors:
Stefan Sagmeister,
Matthias Ernstberger
Designers:
Matthias Ernstberger,
Sarah Noellenheidt,
Marion Mayr
Editor:
Scott Marble
Photography:
Matthias Ernstberger,
Arianne Van Lewis,
Krysztof Kociolek
Client:
Columbia University
Software:
Adobe CS

SALTERBAXTER
Annual Review

003

Client:
Ernst & Young
Tools:
QuarkXPress, Adobe
Photoshop
Paper/Materials:
Revive Silk

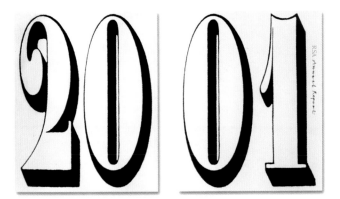

ATELIER WORKS
RSA
Annual Report

004

Art Director:
Ian Chilvers
Designer:
Ian Chilvers
Client:
Royal Society of Arts
Software:
Adobe Photoshop,
QuarkXPress

Fellowship

Diversity has always been the Society's essence: what other institution can claim both Karl Marx and Adam Smith as past members. This tradition continues, and the list of new Fellows from last year includes senior executives and leading figures from Barclays Bank, the British Geological Survey, Carlton TV, the CBI, Charter 88, Commission for Racial Equality, The Economist Group, Ford, The Guardian, The Henley Centre, The Human Fertilisation & Embryology Authority, The New Opportunities Fund, The Financial Times, the Runnymede Trust and Yahoo!. Our Fellowship is both broadly based and hugely influential – it includes half the UK's university vice-chancellors, directors or chief executives from almost every FTSE100 and FTSE250 company, many senior civil servants, cabinet ministers, head teachers, officers in local government and the uniformed services and many more.

But we want the Society to be able to harness the incredible potential of this Fellowship. We have had a website for several years, but we are now seeking to develop it into a powerful networking tool. We intend to connect all our Fellows by, for example, developing an electronic Directory of Fellows, and provide vastly improved access to the RSA and its projects. The new technology will also offer Fellows the opportunity to engage in genuine discussions and the development of new projects, to access the results of all RSA work, and to participate in the governance of the Society as never before. The first stages of the new website should appear early in 2001.

For more details of RSA Fellowship, the new website project or to nominate new Fellows, contact Jon Kudlick, Head of Fellowship, 020 7451 6941 or e-mail Jon.Kudlick@rsa-uk.demon.co.uk

Fellowship of the **RSA** *provides me with another excellent source of new ideas in areas as diverse as education, business and the environment."* Sir Ross Buckland FRSA Chief Executive, Unigate
The way the **RSA** *works means that as a Fellow I get to talk to many people in different fields whom I would never normally meet…"* Nicholas Baldwin FRSA Director, Wroxton College

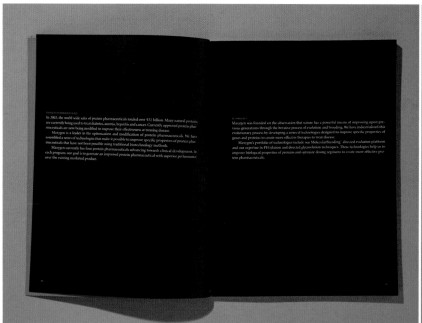

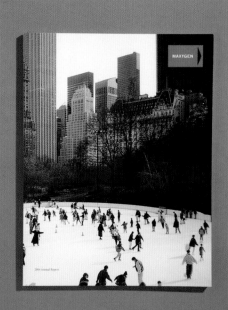

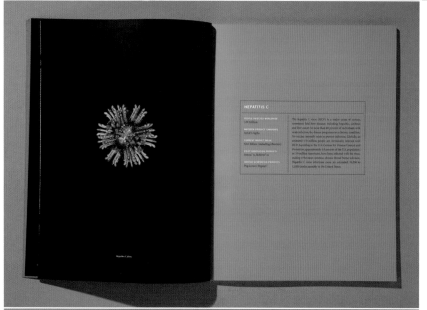

CAHAN
& ASSOCIATES
**Matygen
Annual Report**

005

Art Director:
Bill Cahan
Designer:
Benjamine Morrison
Client:
Matygen
Software:
QuarkXPress,
Adobe Illustrator
Paper/Materials:
80 lb McCoy Matte

TODAY'S PROBLEMS

POSITIVE CHOICES

40%

the percentage of people living in urban areas who put facilities for teenagers at the top of their list of things that need improving in their area

1/3

the proportion of adults saying that teenagers hanging around the streets is a 'big problem' in their area

X2

the increase in anti-social behaviour orders last year

"THE EXTENT OF PERSONAL DEVELOPMENT AND SUBSEQUENT ENHANCED ESTEEM I HAVE WITNESSED BETWEEN THE BEGINNING AND END OF THE (FAIRBRIDGE) PROGRAMME HAS BEEN NOTHING SHORT OF STARTLING."

David Croft, Governor, Her Majesty's Prison Edinburgh

TEENAGERS TARGETED IN DRIVE AGAINST YOB CULTURE

The Times, 20.07.04

IN OCTOBER, THE HOME OFFICE REVEALED THAT THE NUMBER OF ASBOs HANDED OUT IN THE PREVIOUS 12 MONTHS WAS 2,600 – DOUBLE THE NUMBER ISSUED IN THE PREVIOUS FOUR YEARS. OUR HOUSE PROJECT IN CARDIFF ENABLED YOUNG PEOPLE TO POSITIVELY ENGAGE IN THEIR LOCAL COMMUNITY BY RENOVATING A VANDALISED PROPERTY.

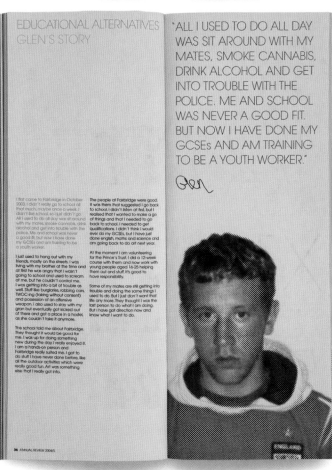

EDUCATIONAL ALTERNATIVES
GLEN'S STORY

"ALL I USED TO DO ALL DAY WAS SIT AROUND WITH MY MATES, SMOKE CANNABIS, DRINK ALCOHOL AND GET INTO TROUBLE WITH THE POLICE. ME AND SCHOOL WAS NEVER A GOOD FIT. BUT NOW I HAVE DONE MY GCSEs AND AM TRAINING TO BE A YOUTH WORKER."

I first came to Fairbridge in October 2003. I didn't really go to school all that much, maybe once a week. I didn't like school, so I just didn't go. All I used to do all day was sit around with my mates, smoke cannabis, drink alcohol and get into trouble with the police. Me and school was never a good fit, but now I have done my GCSEs and am training to be a youth worker.

I just used to hang out with my friends, mostly on the streets. I was living with my brother at the time and at first he was angry that I wasn't going to school and used to scream at me, but he couldn't control me. I was getting into a bit of trouble as well. Stuff like burglaries, robbing cars, TWOC-ing (taking without consent) and possession of an offensive weapon. I also used to stay with my gran but eventually got kicked out of there and got a place in a hostel, as she couldn't take it anymore.

The school told me about Fairbridge. They thought it would be good for me. I was up for doing something new during the day. I really enjoyed it. I am a hands-on person and Fairbridge really suited me. I got to do stuff I have never done before, like all the outdoor activities which were really good fun. Art was something else that I really got into.

The people at Fairbridge were good. It was them that suggested I go back to school. I didn't listen at first, but I realised that I wanted to make a go of things and that I needed to go back to school. I needed to get qualifications. I didn't think I would ever do my GCSEs, but I have just done english, maths and science and am going back to do art next year.

At the moment I am volunteering for the Prince's Trust. I did a 12-week course with them and now work with young people aged 16-25 helping them out and stuff. It's good to have responsibility.

Some of my mates are still getting into trouble and doing the same things I used to do. But I just don't want that life any more. They thought I was the last person to do what I am doing. But I have got direction now and know what I want to do.

NO LAUGHING MATTER

fairbridge Annual Review 2004/5

HAT-TRICK DESIGN
Fairbridge Annual Report

006

Art Director:
Jim Sutherland
Designer:
Adam Giles
Client:
Fairbridge
Software:
QuarkXPress
Paper/Materials:
Sylvan Print

Every dog counts.

Art Director:
Harriet Devoy
Designer:
Steve Royle
Client:
Manchester Dogs'
Home
Software:
QuarkXPress,
Adobe Illustrator,
Adobe Photoshop
Paper/Materials:
Neptune Unique

6,796 dogs

Manchester Dogs' Home Annual Review 2001-2002

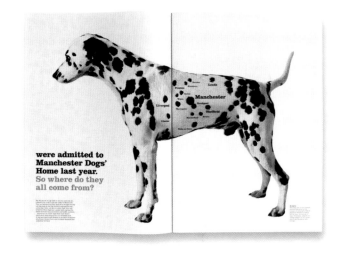

were admitted to
Manchester Dogs'
Home last year.
So where do they
all come from?

9 out of 10 dogs were happily rehomed. That's 5,947 in total.

Chairmans' Report
What have we achieved this year?

BILLY BLUE
CREATIVE, PRECINCT
**City of Sydney
Annual Report**

008

Creative Director:
Mick Thorpe
Art Director:
Justin Smith
Designer:
Justin Smith
Client:
City of Sydney Council
Software:
Adobe Photoshop,
QuarkXPress
Paper/Materials:
Uncoated

CAHAN
& ASSOCIATES
Greater Bay Bancorp
Annual Report

009

Art Directors:
Bill Cahan,
Michael Braley
Designer:
Michael Braley
Client:
Great Bay Bancorp
Software:
QuarkXPress,
Adobe Illustrator
Paper/Materials:
Cougar Opaque 65 lb,
McCoy 80 lb

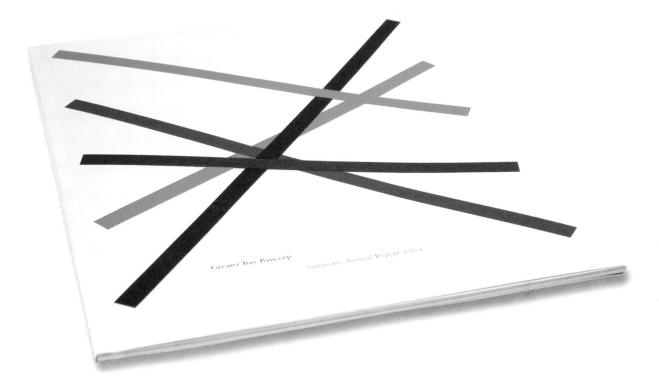

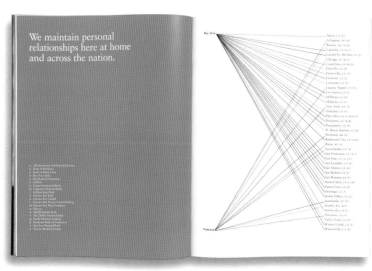

GROUP EARNINGS BEFORE INTEREST AND TAX OF $29.5 MILLION GREW BY 29.4% OVER THE PRIOR PERIOD.

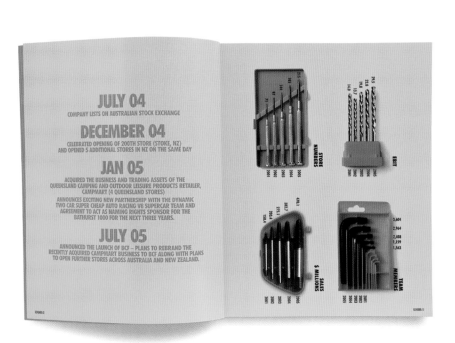

JULY 04
COMPANY LISTS ON AUSTRALIAN STOCK EXCHANGE

DECEMBER 04
CELEBRATED OPENING OF 200TH STORE (STOKE, NZ)
AND OPENED 5 ADDITIONAL STORES IN NZ ON THE SAME DAY

JAN 05
ACQUIRED THE BUSINESS AND TRADING ASSETS OF THE
QUEENSLAND CAMPING AND OUTDOOR LEISURE PRODUCTS RETAILER,
CAMPMART (4 QUEENSLAND STORES)

ANNOUNCES EXCITING NEW PARTNERSHIP WITH THE DYNAMIC
TWO CAR SUPER CHEAP AUTO RACING V8 SUPERCAR TEAM AND
AGREEMENT TO ACT AS NAMING RIGHTS SPONSOR FOR THE
BATHURST 1000 FOR THE NEXT THREE YEARS.

JULY 05
ANNOUNCED THE LAUNCH OF BCF – PLANS TO REBRAND THE
RECENTLY ACQUIRED CAMPMART BUSINESS TO BCF ALONG WITH PLANS
TO OPEN FURTHER STORES ACROSS AUSTRALIA AND NEW ZEALAND.

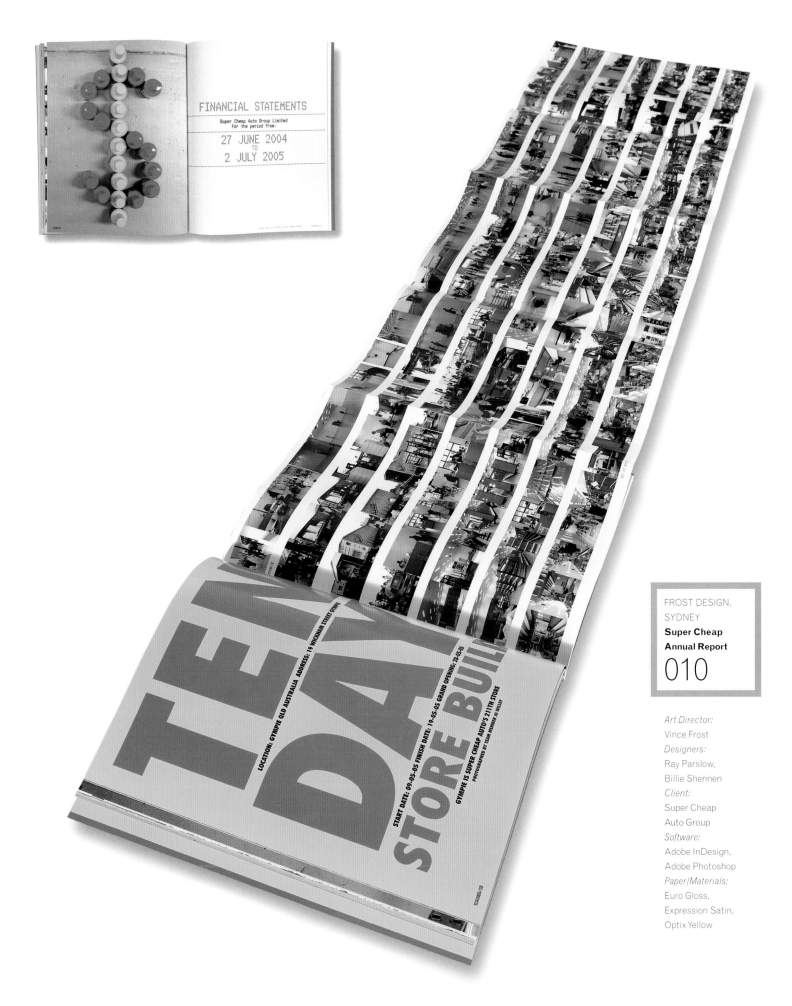

FROST DESIGN,
SYDNEY
**Super Cheap
Annual Report**
010

Art Director:
Vince Frost
Designers:
Ray Parslow,
Billie Shennen
Client:
Super Cheap
Auto Group
Software:
Adobe InDesign,
Adobe Photoshop
Paper/Materials:
Euro Gloss,
Expression Satin,
Optix Yellow

We've done more
than bring back a CEO.
We've brought back
what made Schwab
successful in
the first place.

We sold our
Capital Markets
business to put
the focus back
where it belongs.

Our prices now
are not merely
competitive, but
give us a competitive
advantage.

CAHAN
& ASSOCIATES
Charles Schwab
Annual Report
011

Art Directors:
Bill Cahan,
Sharrie Brooks
Designer:
Sharrie Brooks
Client:
Charles Schwab

THE CHARLES SCHWAB CORPORATION 2004 ANNUAL REPORT

"The Darfur conflict... provoked a wave of shock at the Forum following poignant testimony and the video images projected in the room. We all noted with consternation that despite the strong protest of the international community and the intervention of the African Union, the security and protection of civilians has yet to be guaranteed. The humanitarian crisis remains."

WITNESS Financials 2004*

Open the Eyes of the World
Open the E
Open the E

Audiences Reached

Over the last year, our video productions, media and staff reached audiences of millions worldwide. WITNESS places as much — if not greater importance on the targeted screening of videos before key decision-makers and allies as on the breadth of audiences reached through television, print and online media.

50 key government officials from Paraguay, Senegal, Sierra Leone and the U.S.

80 members of international human rights commissions, intergovernmental bodies, and Truth and Reconciliation Commissions worldwide.

500 NGO representatives and advocates, including partners and other human rights groups from 100 countries.

800 students at schools and universities in the United States via special guest lectures and WITNESS screenings.

2000 individuals through conferences and symposia, with participants representing the worlds of international corporations, philanthropy, technology, and human rights advocacy.

7000 attendees of film festivals and other screenings in Australia, Austria, Canada, Chile, Denmark, Germany, Italy, Netherlands, South Africa, Switzerland, Thailand, the U.S. and elsewhere.

10,000 individuals via targeted distribution and community screenings in Europe, Latin America, Southeast Asia, the U.S. and West Africa.

100,000 radio listeners in Sierra Leone and the U.S.

1,500,000 television viewers in Canada, Ireland, Senegal, Spain, the U.K. and the U.S.

4,000,000 Internet users worldwide.

15,000,000 readers of print media in Argentina, Brazil, Italy, Japan, Korea, Thailand, the U.S. and elsewhere.

LIPPA PEARCE
Witness
Annual Report

012

Art Director:
Harry Pearce
Designer:
Harry Pearce
Client:
Witness, NYC

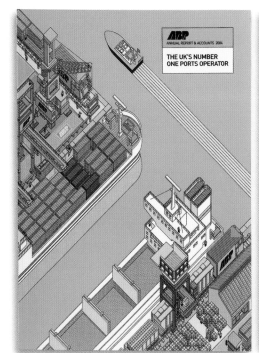

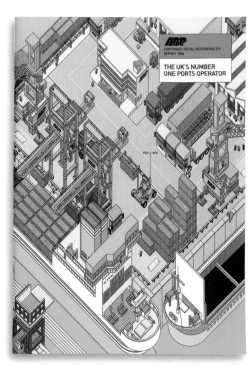

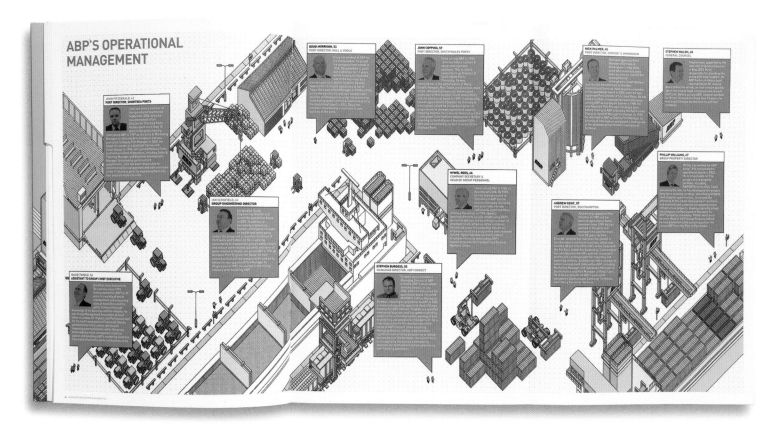

NB:STUDIO
ABP
Annual Report

013

Art Directors:
Nick Finney,
Ben Stott,
Alan Dye
Designer:
Daniel Lock
Client:
Merchant

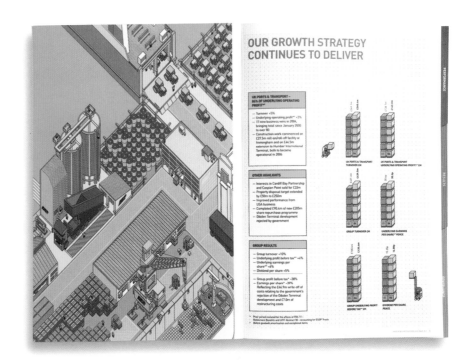

OUR GROWTH STRATEGY CONTINUES TO DELIVER

SMALLER PROJECTS ADD UP TO BIG RETURNS TOO

PORT: HULL
SCHEME:
ADDITIONAL
EXTERNAL
TIMBER STORAGE
COST: £0.6M
LEAD TIME:
5 MONTHS
COMPLETION
DATE: JANUARY
2005

DESCRIPTION:
Second phase of a
£1.1m investment
under a 10-year
agreement with
Marshall Maritime
Services. Phase
one, costing £0.5m,
was completed in
July 2004.

PORT: IPSWICH
SCHEME:
NEW ROLL-ON/
ROLL-OFF BERTH
COST: £6.1M
LEAD TIME:
16 MONTHS
COMPLETION
DATE: JANUARY
2005

DESCRIPTION:
Construction of the
port's second roll-
on/roll-off berth
following a 20-year
agreement with
Ferryways NV to
accommodate
growth in its
Ipswich-Ostend
service.

PORT: GOOLE
SCHEME:
EXPANSION OF
TANK STORAGE
FACILITIES
COST: £0.6M
LEAD TIME:
4 MONTHS
COMPLETION
DATE: FEBRUARY
2005

DESCRIPTION:
Expansion of
facilities for
Kerfoot Group,
which imports
vegetable oil,
mainly for the food
industry. Already a
customer at Goole,
Kerfoot Group is
relocating its
packing and
blending factory
to the port. Under
a 20-year
agreement, £0.6m
is being invested
in buildings,
surfacing and
additional tank
storage.

PORT:
SOUTHAMPTON
SCHEME:
EXTENSION TO
CITY CRUISE
TERMINAL
COST: £0.5M
LEAD TIME:
6 MONTHS
COMPLETION
DATE: MARCH
2005

DESCRIPTION:
Programme of
works to expand
capacity, including
quadrupling the
number of check-
in desks, doubling
the size of the
baggage hall,
increasing the
number of x-ray
machines and
adding additional
long-term parking
spaces and coach
bays. The works
are required to
accommodate the
port's growing
number of cruise
calls.

PORT:
IMMINGHAM
SCHEME:
ASPHALT-
COATING FACILITY
COST: £0.5M
LEAD TIME:
12 MONTHS
COMPLETION
DATE: APRIL 2005

DESCRIPTION:
A facility to
accommodate a
manufacturing
plant for customer
Whitemountain
Roadstone Ltd,
which will be used
to make hot-
coated roadstone
from aggregates
imported from
Norway and
Ireland.

PORT: GARSTON
SCHEME:
AGGREGATES
HANDLING AND
DISTRIBUTION
FACILITY
COST: £0.8M
LEAD TIME:
5 MONTHS
COMPLETION
DATE: MAY 2005

DESCRIPTION:
A 13,000 sq m open
and undercover
storage facility for
the import of
lightweight
aggregates, being
constructed under
an agreement with
Maxit Building
Products Ltd.

PORT: NEWPORT
SCHEME:
EXPANSION OF
STEEL-HANDLING
FACILITIES
COST: £1.4M
LEAD TIME:
11 MONTHS
COMPLETION
DATE: JUNE 2005

DESCRIPTION:
Extension to a
warehousing
facility under a
25-year agreement
with WE Dowds,
to accommodate
growth in its
steel-coil import
business.

PORT: GOOLE
SCHEME:
ADDITIONAL
TIMBER STORAGE
COST: £0.6M
LEAD TIME:
6 MONTHS
COMPLETION
DATE: JUNE 2005

DESCRIPTION:
A 5,000 sq m
extension to
facilities for Global
Shipping Services
Ltd to enable it to
handle additional
volumes of
Russian timber.

PORT:
IMMINGHAM
SCHEME: COAL
STORAGE AND
HANDLING
FACILITIES
COST: £1.7M
LEAD TIME:
5 MONTHS
COMPLETION
DATE: JULY 2005

DESCRIPTION:
Investment in
coal-handling
equipment and
the creation of
an additional
4.5 hectares of
storage facilities.

PORT: GOOLE
SCHEME:
SURFACING OF
STORAGE AREA
COST: £1.3M
LEAD TIME:
6 MONTHS
COMPLETION
DATE: JULY 2005

DESCRIPTION:
Surfacing of
a 9,000 sq m
storage area,
to accommodate
a new Rotterdam
to Goole container
service to be
handled by RMS
Europe.

PORT: SWANSEA
SCHEME:
WAREHOUSE AND
DISTRIBUTION
FACILITY
COST: £1.7M
LEAD TIME:
8 MONTHS
COMPLETION
DATE:
SEPTEMBER 2005

DESCRIPTION:
Development of a
new warehouse
and distribution
facility on the back
of a 15-year
contract with
RKL's Plywood. The
new facility will
include office
accommodation
that will become
RKL's UK
headquarters.

PORT:
TEIGNMOUTH
SCHEME:
REDEVELOPMENT
OF PORT
COST: £4.0M
LEAD TIME:
4 YEARS AND
2 MONTHS
COMPLETION
DATE: 2006

DESCRIPTION:
Major redevelop-
ment to include a
300-metre quay
extension and the
construction of a
3,000 sq m transit
shed, following the
signing of a long-
term agreement
with Mole Valley
Farmers for the
import of agribulks.

MESSAGE FROM THE PRESIDENT

When I sit down with my son and talk about his career plans, or how he views world issues, or… just life, I'm struck by the mind-boggling pace and extent of social change. The world his generation is growing up in is utterly unpredictable. Its distinguishing feature is an incredibly complicated environment of choice. Choice that is more promising, yet more forbidding, than anything my generation faced. What if you could genetically alter your unborn child? What if you had to undergo an eye scan each time you visited a bank, voted, or applied for insurance? What if the world had a CEO? And countries had no borders? These are questions confronted by no previous generation.

18 – 19

IRIDIUM, A DESIGN
AGENCY/KOLEGRAM
SSHRC
Annual Report

014

Art Directors:
Jean-Luc Denat,
Mario L'Écuyer
Designers:
Mario L'Écuyer,
David Daigle
Client:
SSHRC
Software:
QuarkXPress,
Adobe Illustrator,
Adobe Photoshop
Paper/Materials:
Sappi Lustro Dull,
Domtar Cornwall
Pinweave, Rolland
Opaque Smooth

Designers:
Cathy Graham,
Neil Southern
Client:
Durham University
Software:
Adobe Photoshop,
Adobe Illustrator,
QuarkXPress
Paper/Materials:
Munken Lynx

How far
have we come
in the last five years?

Annual Report 2004

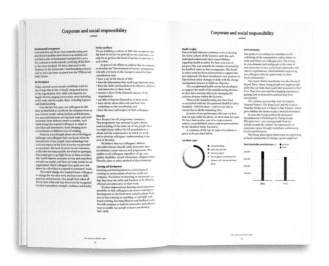

Art Directors:
David Stocks,
Gilmar Wendt
Designer:
Andy Spencer
Client:
MFI Furniture Group
Software:
QuarkXPress
Paper/Materials:
Zen Pure White

Five years ago
MFI was very different from today.
A retail kitchen and bedroom business
selling in the UK and in France.
We carried high debt
and a weak balance sheet.
The outlook was not good.

The business needed to change.

In purely financial terms
we have grown our total sales
from under £800 million
to over £1.5 billion.

So what went wrong
with the implementation
of our supply chain system?

Our investigations have revealed
both technical and
business process problems.
Not insurmountable
but critical to getting the best
out of our new system.

Because of the complexity
of our supply chain
these problems hit us severely.

While we have worked hard
to fix these problems our main focus
above and beyond anything else
has been about improving customer service.

New product introduction was accelerated in the second half of the year – with a focus on lower priced ranges, particularly around the £500 price level. Seven new kitchen ranges, nine new ranges of bedrooms, 15 sofas, seven beds and four bathrooms were introduced. We have closed the gaps in our bed and bedroom ranges, and performance is improving. In 2005, the performance of Hygena kitchens will likewise benefit from lower-end product introductions.

We also increased our advertising spend in the second half to restore our traditional price/value offer with our promotions proposition 'more home for your money'. By the end of the year, independent market research on like-for-like price comparisons showed that our products are now highly price-competitive. We have also made commercial and operational management changes to enable us to get closer to the customer and be able to make faster and better decisions.

In 2004, gross new customer orders were down 3% (by value) on 2003, but net orders were down by 7%. The difference between gross orders and net orders reflects a £36m increase in the level of refunds to customers for missed and late deliveries compared to 2003, primarily due to the supply chain system problems described earlier. This level of refunds is expected to reduce during 2005 as the supply chain system issues are resolved.

The table below shows the opening customer order book for UK Retail, the net orders received in the period (gross customer orders less the value of customer refunds in the period), deliveries (the point at which an order is recorded as a sale) and the closing order book position.

Total orders (excluding VAT)	First half (weeks 52-24) £m		Second half (weeks 25-52) £m		Cumulative (weeks 52-52) £m	
	2003	2004	2003	2004	2003	2004
Opening order book	34	26	90	99	34	26
Net orders	526	490	377	347	903	837
Deliveries	(470)	(417)	(441)	(408)	(911)	(825)
Closing order book	90	99	26	38	26	38

A sale is only recorded as income when the delivery is made to the customer. Orders that were delayed by the supply chain issues have been carried over from 2004 into 2005, resulting in sales of £825m being 9% down on the year, compared to a 7% fall in net orders. The £12m year on year increase in the closing order book is expected to reverse in 2005.

SONSOLES
LLORENS S.L.
Roca
Annual Report

017

Art Director:
Sonsoles Llorens
Designer:
Sonsoles Llorens
Client:
Roca
Software:
Freehand, Adobe
Photoshop

DOPPIO DESIGN
**Australian Hearing
Annual Report**

018

Art Director:
Mauro Bertolini
Designer:
Amber Kadwell
Client:
Australian Hearing
Software:
Adobe Illustrator,
Adobe Photoshop,
Adobe InDesign
Paper/Materials:
Sumo 300 gsm (cover),
135 gsm (text)

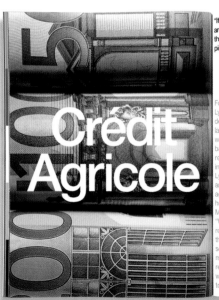

"It's hard to succeed with central policies if you can't see how they are working. With BusinessObjects we can see into every part of the company, at the level of detail that provides the clearest picture." Philippe Méheut, HRIS manager, Crédit Agricole S.A.

Crédit Agricole

For the past five years, the human resource managers of Crédit Lyonnais, one of Europe's largest banks, must have been wondering what could happen next. In 2000, the French government launched a vast social experiment by cutting the national work-week to 35 hours. Then, the euro replaced the French franc—in bank transactions as well as workers' paychecks. Meanwhile, regulators were rewriting the rules for the tightly controlled industry. Just when it seemed things might normalize, Crédit Lyonnais was acquired by Crédit Agricole S.A., requiring yet another major transition. "We had used BusinessObjects to manage our challenges successfully at Crédit Lyonnais," reports human resources information systems (HRIS) manager Philippe Méheut, who took the same position at Crédit Agricole S.A. "When the merger was complete, the new director of human resources said to me, 'We need the same thing here.'" Among the priorities, Crédit Agricole S.A. needed to standardize pay scales, identify people with management potential, and increase mobility for employees within the bank. "The role of human resources is to balance the interests of the company and its workers," Méheut explains. "BusinessObjects is flexible enough to help us do whatever is necessary to succeed in this mission."

CAHAN
& ASSOCIATES
**Business Objects
Annual Report**
019

Art Directors:
Bill Cahan,
Michael Braley
Designer:
Michael Braley
Client:
Business Objects

You make decisions every day.

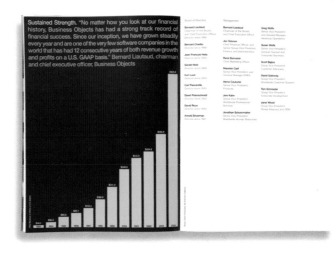

Sustained Strength. "No matter how you look at our financial history, Business Objects has had a strong track record of financial success. Since our inception, we have grown steadily every year and are one of the very few software companies in the world that has had 12 consecutive years of both revenue growth and profits on a U.S. GAAP basis." Bernard Liautaud, chairman and chief executive officer, Business Objects

Defer	Accelerate	Salary	Bonus
Expand	Contract	Europe	Asia
Hire	Fire	Buy	Build
Develop	License	Raise	Lower
Print	Web	Cash	Debt

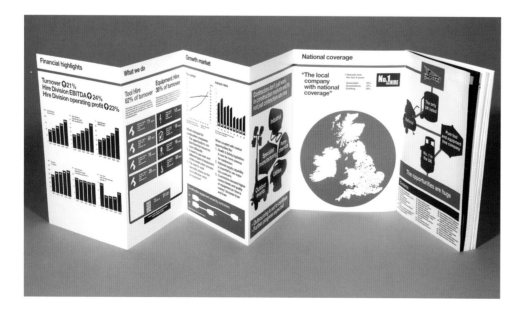

NB:STUDIO
**Speedy Hire
Annual Report**

020

Art Directors:
Nick Finney,
Ben Stott,
Alan Dye
Designer:
Johny Kelly
Client:
Merchant

PENTAGRAM DESIGN,
SAN FRANCISCO
**James Irvine
Annual Reports**

021

Art Director:
Kit Hinrichs
Designers:
Belle How,
David Asari,
Jessica Siegel
Client:
The James Irvine
Foundation
Software:
Adobe InDesign

**How can we maintain a rigorous focus while
remaining adaptable and open to new ideas?**

Foundations are often criticized as rigid institutions that do not adapt quickly to changing circumstances and that stubbornly adhere to their defined agendas. At the same time, foundations are accused of shifting their priorities too often and trying to be all things to all people. In some cases, these seemingly contradictory criticisms are leveled at the same institution.

*"We acknowledge
that solutions are not
developed by the
Foundation in isolation;
rather, they are
crafted in partnership
with our grantees."*

One of the most challenging tasks facing any philanthropic organization is to focus its grantmaking for greatest impact. It is difficult to resist the temptation to do a little of everything, in a quest for breadth and a well-intentioned desire to help. For Irvine, it was taking a close look at this very issue that led the Foundation to reduce its grantmaking agenda from six program areas to three. In doing so, we understood that the areas we have now identified require both patience and sustained investments. We have accordingly made a long-term commitment to these three areas.

In this context, however, how does a foundation ensure that it retains some flexibility and agility to be responsive to a changing environment? Certainly within our program areas, we acknowledge there's a measure of flexibility necessary even with a clear focus. As the environment in which we work shifts, we aim to strike a careful balance between incorporating changes to our agenda without shifting priorities in any fundamental way. We acknowledge that solutions are not developed by the Foundation in isolation; rather, they are crafted in partnership with our grantees. To the extent that we listen carefully, stay attuned to the realities faced by those we seek to serve, and remain receptive to our partners' authentic needs, we will continue to be an adaptable institution.

**How do we demonstrate a sustained commitment to
our grantees as we seek out and embrace new partners?**

In conducting an analysis of our grantmaking over a period of several years, we discovered that three-quarters of our grants each year were awarded to institutions that had a prior relationship with the Irvine Foundation. What were we to make of that? Had we become a closed system with little opportunity for new organizations to receive Irvine funding, or had we demonstrated the importance of sustained, long-term partnership with our grantees? Therein lies the tension, as those who received Irvine support valued the Foundation's sustained partnership, while those who did not receive Irvine funding viewed such data as proof of a closed process.

As we move forward, we remain committed to long-term partnership with our grantees. Moreover, where there is tight alignment between a grantee's core mission and Irvine's program goals, we maintain a predisposition to unrestricted operating support. Of course, such ongoing support will only be provided to those institutions that demonstrate forward progress, organizational effectiveness, and an ability to have positive impact.

At the same time, we are mindful that we want to find additional ways to identify new partners, and we are actively pursuing two concrete strategies to do that. First, after a period of some introspection due to our strategic planning process, our program staff now spends a significant portion of time in the field, not only meeting with prospective partners, but also actively working to identify new prospects for the Foundation's investment. Second, in an effort to broaden our scope, we inaugurated in early 2004 an online application process to provide easy access for organizations, often smaller and not connected to our existing networks, to present their projects and activities to the Foundation, and we have set aside resources to fund such efforts.

*"Where there is tight
alignment between a
grantee's core mission
and Irvine's program
goals, we maintain
a predisposition to
unrestricted operating
support."*

THE JAMES IRVINE FOUNDATION

EXPANDING OPPORTUNITY FOR

THE PEOPLE OF CALIFORNIA

ANNUAL REPORT 2003

ABOUT JAMES IRVINE

A native Californian, James Irvine devoted most of his life to his business interests in San Francisco and the development of his 110,000-acre ranch in Orange County, which he inherited from his father in 1886.

Mr. Irvine believed that significant community responsibility came with his ownership of the ranch, and his philanthropic activities culminated with the formation in 1937 of The James Irvine Foundation. He directed that grants from the Foundation promote the general welfare of the people of California. Mr. Irvine died in 1947.

Since its founding in 1937, the Foundation has made grants totaling more than $800 million for the people of California.

ABOUT THE ILLUSTRATOR

Nicholas Wilton created the illustrations throughout this annual report. A California native, Mr. Wilton is an accomplished illustrator, artist, and teacher. Mr. Wilton attended the College of Creative Studies at the University of California, Santa Barbara, and is a graduate of Art Center College of Design in Los Angeles, a former Irvine Foundation grantee. He lives in northern California with his wife and two daughters.

The Irvine Foundation has supported the arts since its inception and today remains one of the largest funders of the arts in California. We are pleased to be supporting and highlighting the work of one of California's artists in this annual report.

The mission of **The James Irvine Foundation** is to expand opportunity for the people of California to participate in a vibrant, successful, and inclusive society. In pursuit of this mission, the Foundation is guided by the following goals: **Advance** the educational and economic prospects of low-income Californians to create and share in the state's prosperity; **Engage** a broad cross-section of Californians in the civic and cultural life of their communities and the state; **Enhance** mutual understanding and communications among diverse racial, ethnic, and socioeconomic groups; and **Enrich** the state's intellectual and creative environment.

CORPORATE

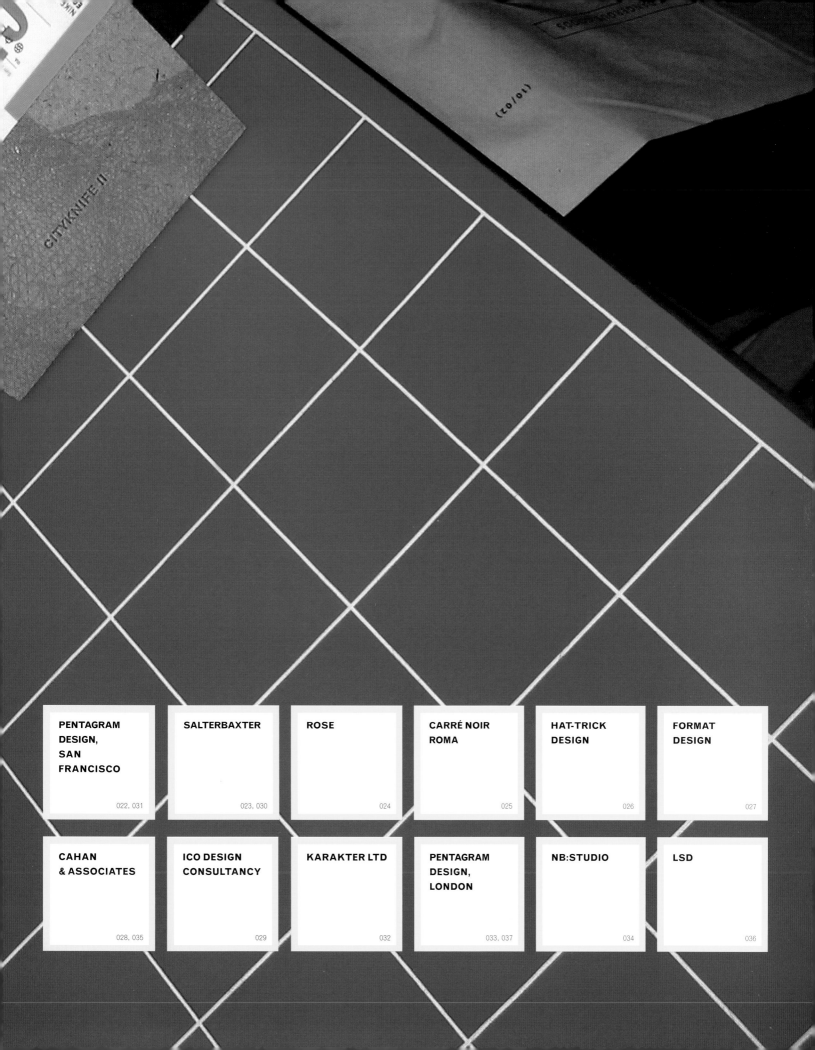

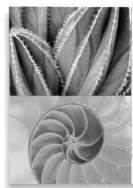

You face them every day. Cream or sugar? Stairs or elevator? Paper or plastic? At the risk of adding to life's tough choices, we bring you the 2006 Safeco Conference of Champions. It's our way of thanking the top 350 Safeco agents for all they do to help make our business a success. And we'd like you to be among that select number. So, accelerate your drive and amplify your passion. A trip for your memory books is up ahead.

Where are we pointing our compass next year? In two different, yet equally enticing directions. For the top 100 Safeco agents, your destination will be Kona-Kohala Coast on the Big Island of Hawaii. Now, this isn't the Hawaii you may already know. This is the Hawaii that only a privileged few have ever experienced. The Hawaii of beachfront bungalows, private championship golf courses, secluded open-air spas, and hushed-tone service. It's the Hawaii of the exclusive Four Seasons Resort Hualalai at Historic Ka'upulehu.

Rated by many, including *Travel & Leisure* magazine, as one of the most magnificent escapes in the world, its elegance is surpassed only by its splendor. Which may explain the celebrities you're likely to spot nibbling taro chips under a seaside lanai. Our other deserving group of agents gets to turn their sights to New Mexico and the Hyatt Regency Tamaya Resort and Spa. Set along the Rio Grande at the foothills of the Sandia Mountains, this getaway melds ancient pueblo culture with modern luxuries for a journey you'll never forget. Your ticket to join us is entirely in your hands. Good luck. Stay focused. We'll be pulling for you.

PENTAGRAM DESIGN, SAN FRANCISCO
Safeco Choices

022

Art Director:
Kit Hinrichs
Designer:
Ashlie Benton
Client:
Safeco
Software:
Adobe InDesign
Paper/Materials:
Sappi McCoy, Cougar

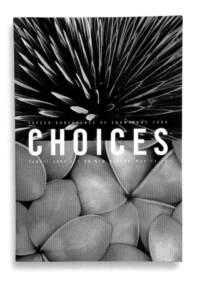

CHOICES

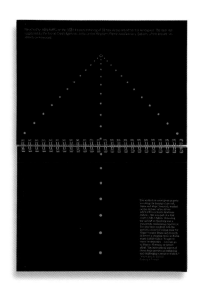

Bright
enough?

DentonWildeSapte...

Brilliant people,
real teamwork,
high profile clients,
great training,
a sparkling future.

Brilliant
people...

SALTERBAXTER
**Graduate Recruit-
ment Brochure**

023

Art Director:
Salterbaxter
Designer:
Salterbaxter
Client:
Denton Wilde Sapte
Software:
QuarkXPress,
Photoshop
Paper/Materials:
Challenger Offset

International Business
Sir Bob Reid

Understanding the importance of appreciating and respecting different international cultures is paramount to doing business in today's society. This is Sir Bob Reid's lesson, in which he shows that the world's plethora of cultures need to be properly observed: both out of respect, and also to enable business to be conducted efficiently.

He draws on his time in West Africa and Thailand to make his point. The West Africans were ebullient, outgoing and keen on provoking discussion as a means of getting to know someone: "They look for a contention so you can argue something through, and in the course of that argument they grow to like you."

This was in stark contrast to Thailand, where society dictated a completely different approach. There, studied pragmatism in a much lower key was required. "Nothing happens quickly, you make sure, whereas the Nigerians want it to happen tomorrow."

Understanding the subtleties of different cultures' mannerisms and behaviour is crucial, with business leaders needing to be sensitive to adapting in their company. Reid relates the tale of two Nigerian friends who went to Japan expecting to tie up their business in a quick meeting by telling the Japanese what to do.

The Japanese, bemused by an approach that was so at odds with their own culture, did not respond well. The Nigerians returned despondent, saying: "We don't understand these people." Reid recalls answering: "That's not the point; they don't understand you. That's much more important."

Going from one society to another requires understanding, learning and an ability to adapt. "You can't import your own philosophies and your own processes into a situation in which these could well be found to be alien."

His advice is to spend time listening, watching, and seeing how far past experiences can help in a new situation. "You must take time to understand what you are in, what are the norms of that situation, and then you make your adaptability after you've listened and learnt for some time."

Managing Failure
John Lundgren

Failure is an essential, valuable learning experience in business, and we can all learn from our mistakes. It is how we manage this failure that is the central tenet of John Lundgren's lesson.

To him, exploring and pushing the boundaries in business plays an important part in the learning process, and a manager who is too risk averse does not fully challenge himself, his organisation or the team around him.

Lundgren's lesson for managing failure is simple: "Failures can be pretty valuable learning experiences, and not all that costly, especially if prior to the failure, there's a reasonable contingency in place."

He cites Georgia-Pacific's approach in Europe as a good example of how to learn from failure and minimise risk. At each stage of development in an emerging market, the company meticulously plans and measures its progress – but sometimes external forces scupper these well-laid preparations. In Poland, for example, despite having three-years' worth of experience and a dedicated sales force, Georgia-Pacific was forced to draw the conclusion that the market was already being adequately served, and it was not adding enough value to warrant staying there. "It wasn't a fun thing to do but we learnt, we closed the sales office, we're no longer in Poland," he says.

In his lesson, Lundgren advises how to view such circumstances objectively. Rather than concluding that an episode has ended in failure, his advice is to look at it from a different angle, learn from the experience, and realise that a move into another area making better use of the skillset at hand might be pragmatic.

In this way, failure does not have to be final. Lundgren believes all that's needed is "a logical, rational look at why you've failed, what you've learned from it, take that to your next experience, and then it's not such a bad failure."

ROSE
**Fifty Lessons,
Daedalus Edition**

024

Art Directors:
Simon Elliott,
Garry Blackburn
Designer:
Simon Elliott
Client:
Fifty Lessons
Software:
QuarkXPress
Paper|Materials:
GF Smith Colorplan

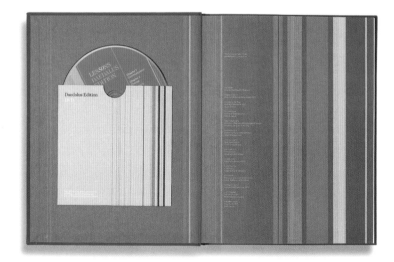

Art Director:
Massimiliano Sagrati
Designer:
Hanna Lehtinen
Client:
Coesia Group-
Bologna, Italy
Software:
Adobe Illustrator,
QuarkXPress
Paper|Materials:
Fedrigoni Tatami, Sirio

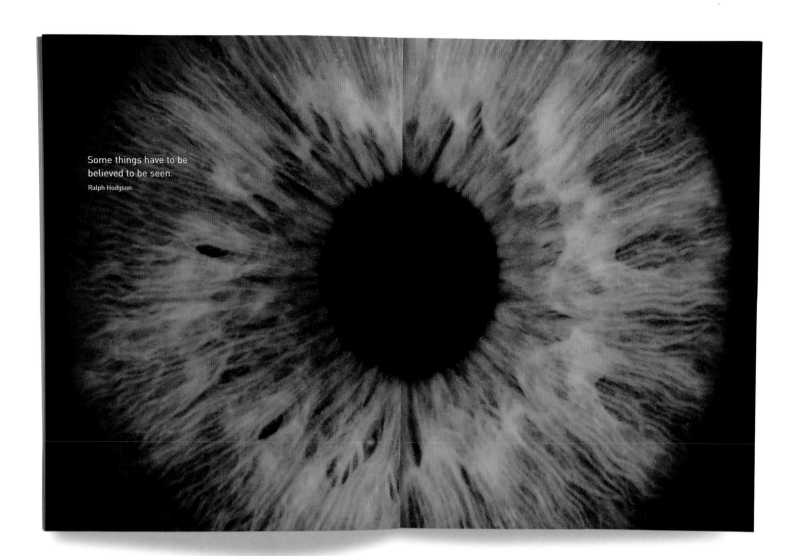

Some things have to be
believed to be seen.
Ralph Hodgson

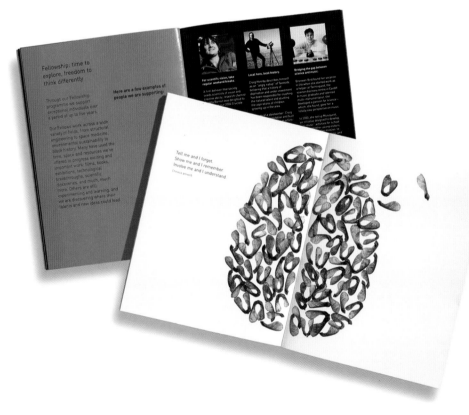

If one is lucky, a solitary
fantasy can totally transform
one million realities.
Maya Angelou

HAT-TRICK DESIGN
**Nesta Learning
Program (Set of 3)**

026

Art Director:
Jim Sutherland
Designer:
Jim Sutherland
Client:
Nesta
Software:
QuarkXPress

FORMAT DESIGN
**Latham & Watkins
LLP Image
Brochure**
027

Art Director:
Knut Ettling
Designer:
Knut Ettling
Client:
Latham & Watkins LLP
Software:
Adobe InDesign

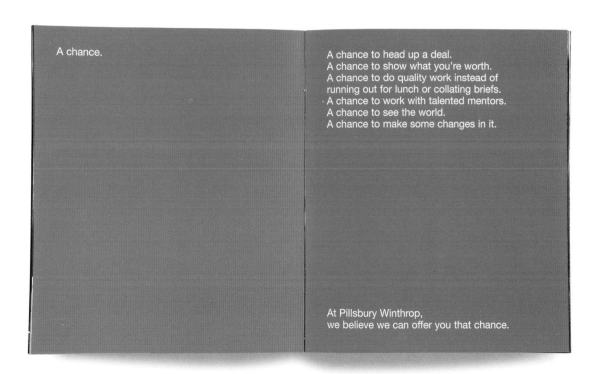

A chance.

A chance to head up a deal.
A chance to show what you're worth.
A chance to do quality work instead of
running out for lunch or collating briefs.
A chance to work with talented mentors.
A chance to see the world.
A chance to make some changes in it.

At Pillsbury Winthrop,
we believe we can offer you that chance.

CAHAN
& ASSOCIATES
**Pillsbury Winthrop
Recruitment**

028

Art Director:
Bill Cahan
Designers:
David Stolberg,
Michael Braley
Client:
Pillsbury Winthrop
Shaw Pittman

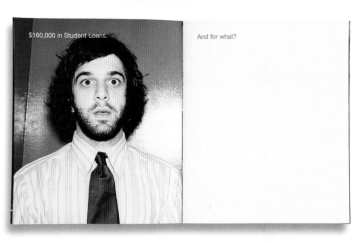

REACT LISTEN

There are two levels of emergency:

Level 1
Await further instructions

You will hear an

intermittent fire alarm

or an

announcement over the PA system telling you to

await further instructions

Level 2
Evacuate immediately

You will hear a

continuous fire alarm

or an

announcement over the PA system telling you to

evacuate immediately

ICO DESIGN
CONSULTANCY
**Emergency
Evacuation Manual**
029

Art Director:
Vivek Bhatia
Designers:
Vivek Bhatia,
Akira Chatani
Client:
Rolls Royce
Software:
Adobe InDesign
Paper/Materials:
Accent

REACT WAIT

At the assembly point:
Report any information to your fire marshal

Await further instructions

Do not walk away

Do not attempt to re-enter Buckingham Gate

Follow the instructions of the emergency services

Wait where instructed

If you have your mobile with you, keep it switched on

Do not attempt to call the office

Go home immediately if instructed

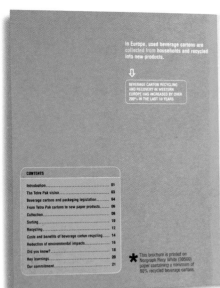

In Europe, used beverage cartons are collected from households and recycled into new products.

⇩

BEVERAGE CARTON RECYCLING AND RECOVERY IN WESTERN EUROPE HAS INCREASED BY OVER 200% IN THE LAST 10 YEARS.

Introduction

Recycling of beverage cartons in Europe
In 2003, the beverage carton industry achieved 30% recycling and 58% total recovery' of all carton packaging in the previous European Union of 15 member states. During the same period, the enlarged European Union of 25 member states achieved 28% recycling and 53% total recovery. Beverage cartons can be recycled into new paper products such as office stationery, tissue paper, cardboard, corrugated board and paper bags.

'Total recovery excludes both recycling and energy recovery.

Sharing our recycling experience worldwide
At Tetra Pak we are committed to achieving a 25% recycling rate worldwide for our used carton packages by the end of 2008. While there is no legal demand for recycling in most countries outside Europe, we have set ourselves this target to make a positive contribution to the communities we serve.

Around the world, Tetra Pak works with stakeholders to develop local collection and recycling programmes. We employ over 100 professionals dedicated to environmental issues.

IN 2003, THE TOTAL RECYCLING RATE OF BEVERAGE CARTONS IN THE EUROPEAN MARKET (EU15) WAS

30%

* This brochure is printed on Norgraph Recy White (30500) paper containing a minimum of 80% recycled beverage cartons.

CONTENTS

Introduction 01
The Tetra Pak vision 03
Beverage cartons and packaging legislation 04
From Tetra Pak cartons to new paper products 06
Collection 08
Sorting 10
Recycling 12
Costs and benefits of beverage carton recycling 14
Reduction of environmental impacts 16
Did you know? 18
Key learnings 20
Our commitment 21

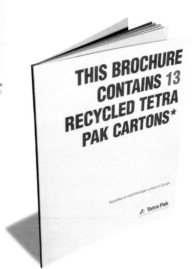

THIS BROCHURE CONTAINS 13 RECYCLED TETRA PAK CARTONS*

Recycling of used beverage cartons in Europe

Tetra Pak

SALTERBAXTER
Recycling Brochure

030

Art Director:
Salterbaxter
Designer:
Salterbaxter
Client:
Tetra Pak
Software:
QuarkXPress
Paper/Materials:
Made from recycled beverage cartons

⇨ **Sorting**

Since beverage cartons are collected together with other packaging types from households, sorting is needed in many cases to separate different materials or paper grades for recycling.

The European List of Standard Grades of Recovered Paper and Board defines used beverage carton as a tradable waste paper grade (EN 643 5 03 00: Polyethylene coated used liquid packaging board, with or without aluminium, containing a minimum of 50% fibres).

The EN 643 Standard is published by the European Paper Industry and the European Standardisation Organisation (CEN). Therefore, they can be sent from one EU member state to another for recycling in paper mills according to the EU Waste Shipment Regulation.

Tetra Pak cartons collected with mixed paper or paper packaging
Beverage cartons represent less than 1% of all waste paper collected in Europe and less than 5% of all paper packaging put on the market in Europe.

Tetra Pak cartons collected from households in an appropriate paper container are either sent to a paper sorting centre or are baled and sent directly to a paper mill. This waste paper is typically separated into newsprint, corrugated board and mixed paper. Generally beverage cartons remain with the mixed paper grade for recycling if they represent less than 5% of the total.

In Sweden however, where used beverage cartons represent up to 35% of the paper packaging collected, they are recycled together with the other paper packaging without any sorting.

Separating Tetra Pak cartons from lightweight packaging
In countries where beverage cartons are collected in the same container as plastic bottles and cans, the different materials must be separated either manually or automatically before being sent to recycling plants.

470,000

BALES (WEIGHING 600 KG EACH) OF USED BEVERAGE CARTONS WERE SENT TO PAPER MILLS IN 2003 (EU 25)

10

11

Information is the engine of your business, and you need to ensure that it is always secure and always available throughout your enterprise. That's why Symantec's approach to information management is designed to simultaneously provide world-class security and world-class administration of your network resources. We call the result information integrity. It is a revolutionary new approach to information management designed to help keep your business up, running, and growing, no matter what happens.

PENTAGRAM DESIGN,
SAN FRANCISCO
Symantec
Brochures
031

Art Director:
Kit Hinrichs
Designer:
Erik Schmitt
Client:
Symantec Corporation
Software:
Adobe InDesign
Paper/Materials:
Sappi McCoy

Content

Viability – the main theme

The centennial visual profile

KARAKTER LTD
**Hydro Centennial
Site Menu
Brochure**
032

Art Director:
Clive Rohald
Client:
Norsk Hydro

A viable society. A need. An idea. 36,000 pr...
Energy. Cooperation. Aluminium. Determina...
boundaries. Respect. Nature. Courage. 100...

Progress of a different nature.

Celebrating the Hydro Centennial

PENTAGRAM
DESIGN, LONDON
**J P Morgan
Corporate Brochure**

033

Art Director:
John Rushworth
Client:
J P Morgan
Illustrator:
Aude Van Ryn

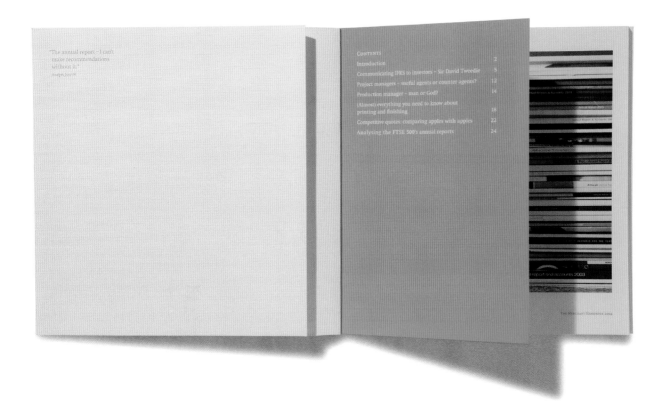

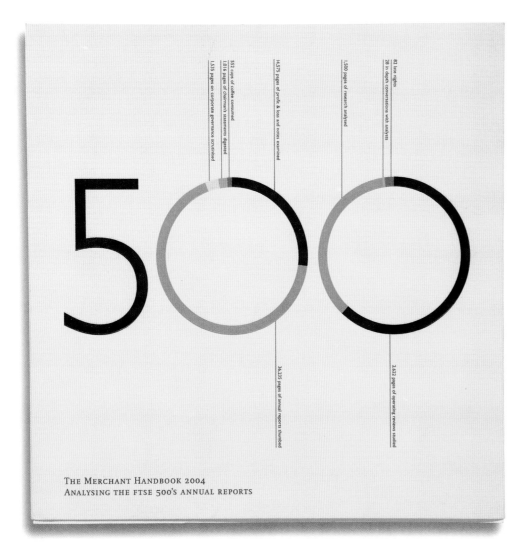

NB:STUDIO
The Merchant Handbook

034

Art Directors:
Nick Finney,
Ben Stott,
Alan Dye
Designer:
Sarah Fullerton
Client:
Merchant

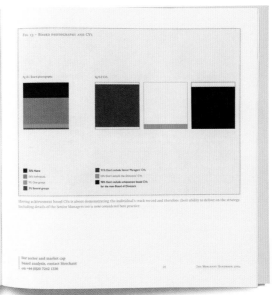
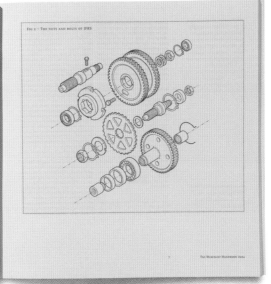

CAHAN
& ASSOCIATES
Lubri-Loy
Corporate Brochure
035

Art Directors:
Bill Cahan,
Michael Braley
Designer:
Michael Braley
Client:
Lubri-Loy
Software:
QuarkXPress,
Adobe Illustrator,
Adobe Photoshop
Paper/Materials:
Century Matte 80 lb

Lubri-Loy's primary aim is to

fight friction.

Since 1949, Lubri-Loy has been producing products that handle the spectrum of situations—from the most extreme conditions to the very basic, everyday maintenance. Lubri-Loy can lower your operating costs, maximize efficiency, increase power and decrease maintenance downtime.

From engines to gear boxes to all mechanical parts, machinery requires ongoing lubrication, fortification and enhancement to survive and continue working to maximum capacity. But a basic lubricant, fortifier or fuel enhancer simply won't accomplish your needs over the short or long term.

In this, our sixth decade, Lubri-Loy—a blend of the terms lubricant and alloy—distributes an array of superior lubricant, fortifier and fuel enhancing products in more than 35 countries on five continents.

Headquartered in St. Louis, Missouri, Lubri-Loy's technology serves a wide range of markets including the industrial, metal fabrication, railroad, agriculture, construction, automotive, utility, trucking and marine industries.

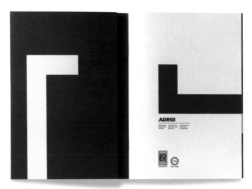

LSD
Corporate
Brochure

036

Art Director:
Gabriel Martínez
Designers:
Gabriel Martínez,
Paz Martín
Client:
Adegi
Software:
Freehand
Paper/Materials:
Offset

Industrial Practice Group
New Challenges for Traditional Industries

PENTAGRAM
DESIGN, LONDON
Egon Zehnder
Corporate Brochure

037

Art Director:
John Rushworth
Client:
Egon Zehnder

Our unique management assessment process, combined
with our global executive search capability, enables
the Egon Zehnder International Industrial Practice Group
to consistently bring our clients the most promising
leaders in the automotive, energy, utilities, mining, natural
resources, chemicals and other process industries.

In this new era of competition, these industries are
being transformed by powerful forces – deregulation,
privatization, emerging markets, B2B consortiums,
and mega-mergers – that will change every aspect
of doing business.

ENERGY

GAS

ELECTRICITY

OIL

Our industry calls for leaders who have the competence and intellectual agility to clear a series of unique competitive hurdles.

1

Understanding Industry Challenges

In newly deregulated markets, executives must be able both to retain and build market share by offering innovative services and products, while managing costs by pursuing aggressive international purchasing strategies. In newly privatized markets, executives must exercise commercial mind-sets and entrepreneurial drive to enable their companies to compete and thrive.

Established companies expanding into emerging markets must rapidly build entirely new local management teams with the right industry experience and functional skills. Companies forming or participating in B2B consortiums require executives who understand all the short- and long-term benefits and risks of these relationships.

To fully reap the anticipated benefits of large mergers, the merging companies must appreciate the strengths and weaknesses of all the executives in the new entity.

Egon Zehnder International's Industrial Practice Group commands a unique global view across industries and functions that enables you to meet and manage these challenges with confidence.

5

2

Who We Are and How We Are Unique to Our Profession

Though top-tier executive search firms often seem comparable, Egon Zehnder International is unique.

3

ASSEMBLY

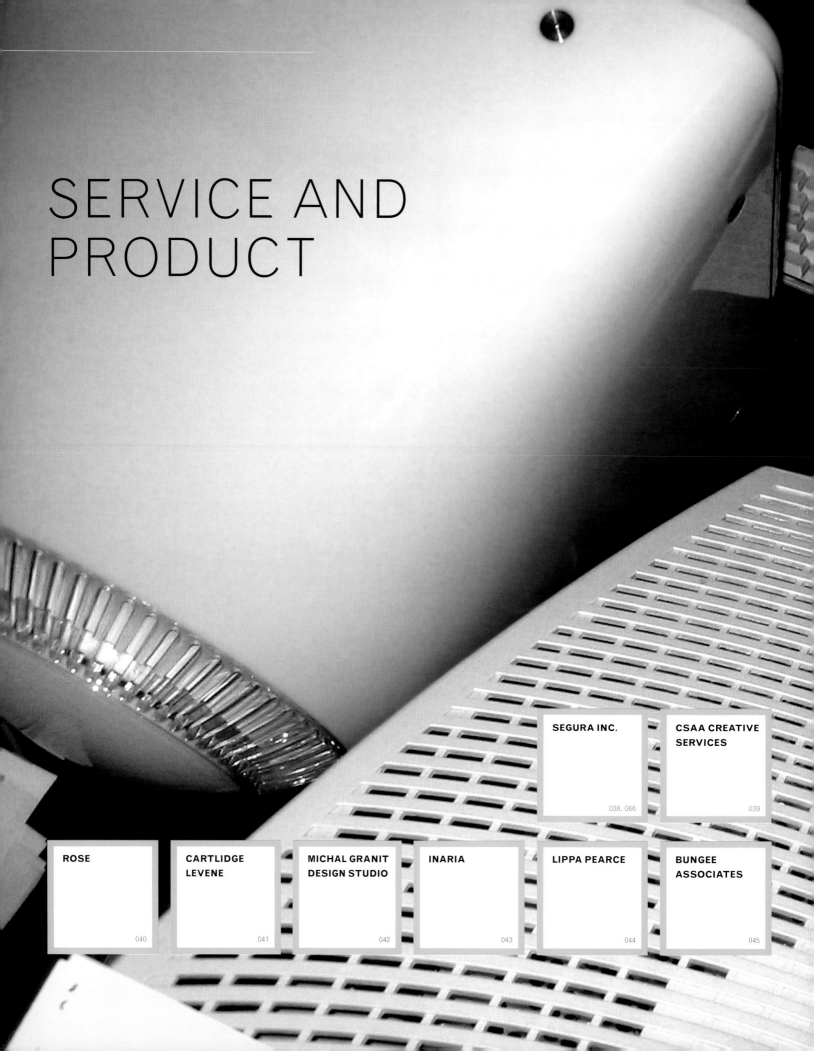

SERVICE AND
PRODUCT

SEGURA INC.
Crop (Large Size Brochure)

038

Art Director:
Carlos Segura
Designers:
Carlos Segura,
Dave Weik,
Chris May,
Tnop
Client:
Corbis
Software:
Adobe InDesign,
Adobe Photoshop,
Adobe Illustrator

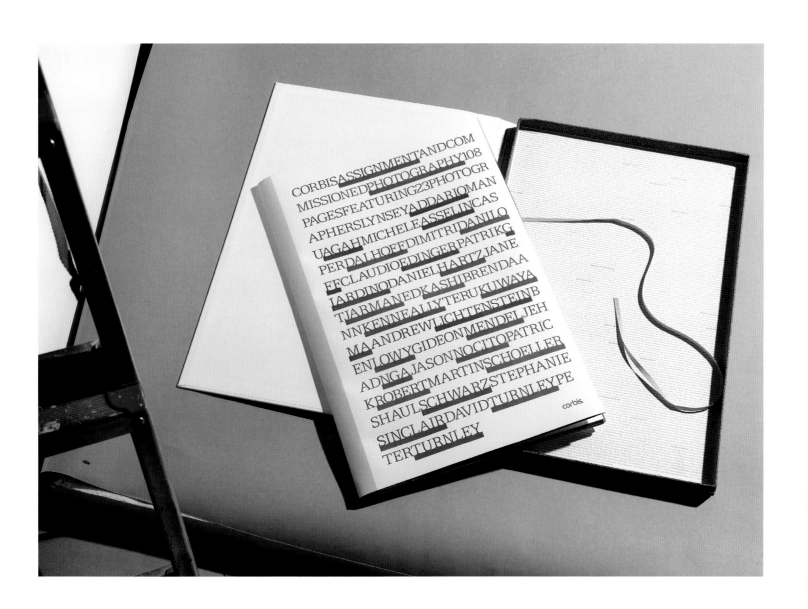

Wield your superpowers wisely.

What the program is:
- Front-line employee empowerment
- A change in operating policy and procedures
- A way to add value to our relationship with our Members and for employees
- A way to create opportunity for our business and for employees

What it is not:
- A promotional campaign
- A gift to our Members
- A way to please every Member, every time
- An expense account

What you can give:
Use your creativity and resources to identify gestures of varied potential. Here are some examples to guide your team:
- Removal of one Emergency Road Service event
- Membership enrollment, dues, or upgrade waiver
- Removal of a $10 returned check charge

What you cannot give:
- Changes to payment terms
- Changes to Membership by-laws
- Changes to rates upon which insurance premiums are based
- Changes to premium amounts or policy reinstatement

Accountability
Each front-line employee will be empowered to provide gestures up to $100 in value without management approval. Giving gestures is not an exact science. Sometimes it requires sizing up a situation and making a judgment call. Along the way managers and/or supervisors will be there for you, discussing the actions you've taken, offering guidance, and overseeing your monthly performance report. Together you will help to ensure that AAA's new empowerment policy is working the way it is intended to work.

Even superheroes need a little guidance now and then.

Let's see to it that Members always come first.

About your new superpowers:

Front-line employees, like you, have been telling us lately that you'd like more power. But not just any powers ... special powers. Congratulations! Your super-signal was received and you now have the ability to create the most loyal and satisfied customers in the entire universe.

Wield your new power wisely: ask yourself the following questions before offering a AAA goodwill gesture. Interestingly enough, they're the same questions that managers used to ask themselves before granting approval. The difference is you can do it better, stronger, and faster.

Question One:
Is the solution good for business?

Consider the potential effect on our business of a Member's dissatisfaction. Is this a Member we should make a special effort to keep? Factors like the depth of a Member's relationship with AAA and the number of years he or she has been a Member can signal the importance of a little extra attention.

For example, a 15-year Member who insures both home and auto with us, and who frequently books trip through Travel Services, is a very valuable Member. It would make sense to increase the value of a goodwill gesture for a Member like this. On the other hand, if a Member makes frequent Emergency Road Service calls and insurance claims or if they have a history of payments returned by the bank, he or she may actually be costing us money and making a gesture of any sort may be inappropriate.

In the end, it comes down to how much benefit a Member offers AAA. In other words, do they deserve a superhero's rescue?

*You've broken free of irksome approvals.
Now go make the world a better place.*

CSAA CREATIVE
SERVICES
**Your New Super-
powers Booklet**

039

Art Director:
Virginia Vovchuk
Designer:
Jeff Carino
Client:
CSAA Sales & Service
Software:
Adobe InDesign
Paper/Materials:
Starwhite Vicksburg
(Fox River)

ROSE
**Elwin Street
Publishing
Catalog**

040

Art Director:
Simon Elliott
Designer:
Simon Elliott
Client:
Elwin Street
Software:
QuarkXPress,
Adobe Photoshop
Paper/Materials:
Hello Satin 170 gsm

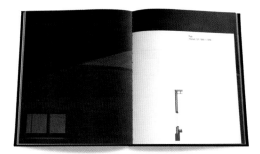

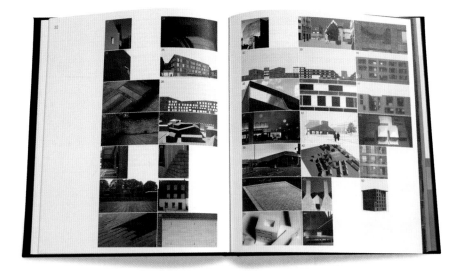

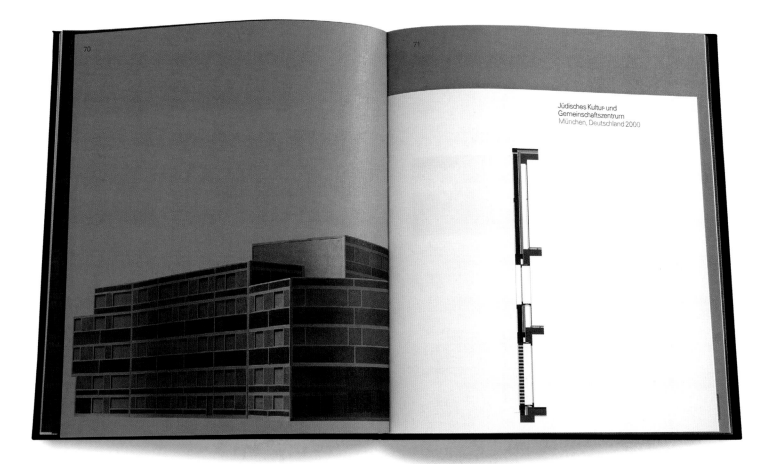

Art Director:
Ian Cartlidge
Designer:
Hector Pottie
Client:
Sergison Bates/GTA
Software:
Adobe InDesign
Paper/Materials:
Cloth-bound with
failblocked text and
printed inlay (cover),
GF Smith Aria (text)

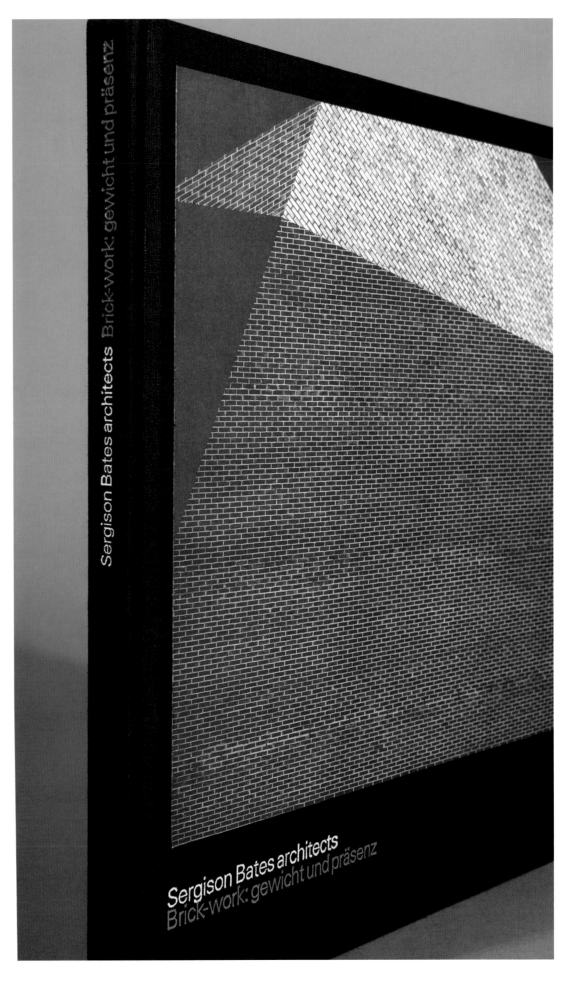

MICHAL GRANIT
DESIGN STUDIO
Fashion Catalog

042

Art Director:
Michal Granit
Illustrator:
Orit Bergman
Client:
Comme il faut
Software:
Freehand,
Adobe Photoshop

Art Directors:
Andrew Thomas,
Debora Berardi
Designers:
Andrew Thomas,
Debora Berardi
Client:
One & Only Resorts
Paper/Materials:
Garda Pat 13 (text),
Color Plan Bagdad
Brown (cover)

Mexico

One&Only Palmilla

Art Director:
Harry Pearce
Designer:
Harry Pearce
Client:
"26"

BUNGEE
ASSOCIATES
Excursions
Catalog
045

Art Director:
Joe Tjiam
Designer:
Gwendoline Ng
Client:
Air Division Pte Ltd
Software:
Adobe Photoshop,
Freehand,
QuarkXPress
Paper/Materials:
Conqueror Wove
White and Natural

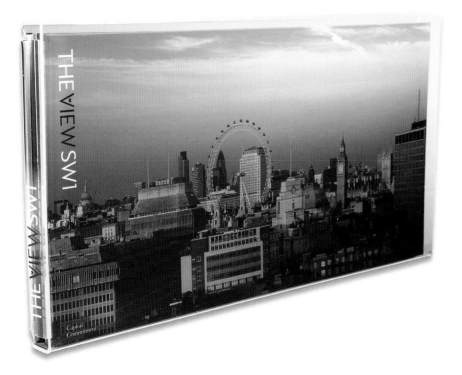

HAT-TRICK DESIGN
The View SW1

046

Art Directors:
Jim Sutherland,
David Kimpton
Designers:
David Kimpton,
Adam Giles
Client:
Land Securities
Software:
QuarkXPress

While the harbour, its ferries, the bridge, and
our beaches are indelibly sculpted into Sydney's
character, the face of the city is changing.
Here on the city's western foreshore there's a new enthusiasm, a new vigour,
a new way of looking at business – and at its heart is King Street Wharf. Along the
western foreshore complexes of influence are flocking to the harbour's edge – at
The Island, the adjacent stylish Bay, and along the length of Hickson Road. Each has
been drawn by the precinct's irresistible allure – its proximity to the city and its
abundant lifestyle and transport options. Here the harbour, the sea, and the vitality of
the city are bringing our sense of perspective alive. Here at Dupain,
you are effortlessly connected.

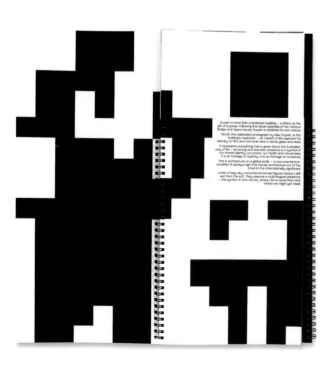

Dupain is more than a landmark building – it offers us the
gift of surprise. Following the heroic example of the Harbour
Bridge and Opera House, Dupain is destined for icon status.

'Bondi', the celebrated photograph by Max Dupain, is the
building's inspiration – an instant of life captured for
eternity on film, and now built here in stone, glass and steel.

It represents everything that is great about the Australian
way of life – its strong and dramatic presence is a symbol of
our shared identity, our power, our health and robustness.
It is an homage to Sydney. And an homage to ourselves.

This is architecture on a global scale – a monumental icon
amplified 15 storeys high that moves architecture out of the
trivial to the internationally significant.

Under a hazy sky, monumental tanned figures beckon, still
wet from the surf. They assume a mythological presence
– the symbol of who we are, where we've come from and
– the symbol of who we are, where we might yet head.

FROST DESIGN,
SYDNEY
**Dupain Property,
Marketing Brochure**
047

Art Director:
Vince Frost
Designer:
Kasia Wydrowski
Client:
Australand/Multiplex
Software:
Adobe InDesign,
Adobe Photoshop,
Adobe Illustrator
Paper/Materials:
Mohawk superfine

THERE

Interchangeable Industry Sector Brochures

048

Art Director:
There
Designer:
There
Client:
Suters Architects
Software:
Adobe InDesign,
Adobe Illustrator,
Adobe Photoshop
Paper/Materials:
Uncoated and coated
paper stocks

FLORE VAN RYN
Catalog / First Collection Wild-spirit Furnitures
049

Art Director:
Flore Van Ryn
Designer:
Flore Van Ryn
Client:
Wildspirit
Software:
Adobe InDesign
Paper/Materials:
Coated matte 350 gsm
(cover), 150 gsm (text)

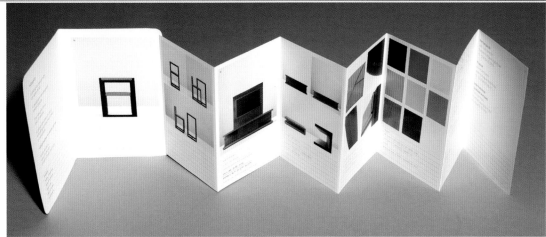

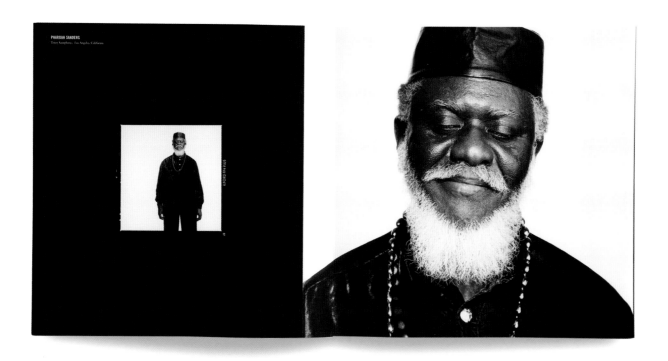

PHARAOH SANDERS
Tenor Saxophone, Los Angeles, California

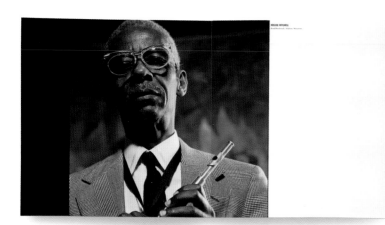

ROSCOE MITCHELL
Reed/Woodwind, Madison, Wisconsin

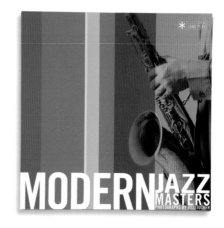

*LONG PLAY

MODERN JAZZ MASTERS
PHOTOGRAPHS BY BILL TUCKER

HAMIET BLUIETT
Baritone Saxophone, New York, New York

Portraits of the Other Music

In my youth I saw alchemists, magicians, saints, downright holy men not like "oh my Lord", but "Lord have mercy". Drenched in spirit, these cats had the Holy Ghost like right now.

The reach and impact of this music, sometimes labeled free jazz, the new thing, avant garde, fire music, experimental or great blackness, has developed a much larger audience than what general media would have one believe. The music and its players are known in practically every country on earth. That's why the artists in this beautiful book are considered true pioneers and soldiers of the cause.

We are unquestionably heirs to the enormous legacy of Scott Joplin, Jelly Roll Morton, Louis Armstrong, Duke Ellington, Fletcher Henderson, Charlie Parker, Dizzy Gillespie, Thelonious Monk, Charles Mingus, John Coltrane, Miles Davis, Ornette Coleman and Sun Ra along with hundreds of other known and unknown giants of creative music.

The artists mentioned above I would call system deliverers. They are both spirit and conduit to the entire history of 20th century music. They were each able to change something about this world with their music. The life in the music expresses foremost a need for exploration. It is creativity in all of its profound intelligence, immediacy, rawness, and realness. Each of these photos reflects the energy of the improviser in a variety of moods. Bluiett, Malachi Favors, Billy Bang, Roscoe Mitchell, Fareed Haque, Ari Brown, Pharoah Sanders, Leo Smith, Cecil Payne are all cats that I truly love. I have the highest respect for their music and cultural contributions.

HARTFORD DESIGN, INC.
Jazz Masters Promotion

050

Art Director:
Tim Hartford
Designers:
Lisa Ermatinger,
Judith Miller
Client:
Nimrod Systems
Software:
QuarkXPress
Paper/Materials:
Potlatch McCoy

Art Director:
Stefan Sagmeister
Designer:
Ariane Spanari
Client:
Anni Kuan
Software:
Adobe CS
Paper/Materials:
Newsprint,
gold pieces

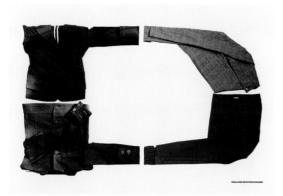

ANNI KUAN
HAPPILY INVITES YOU TO PREVIEW THE
FALL AND WINTER 2005 COLLECTION AT
THE FASHION COTERIE FROM SUNDAY,
FEB 27TH TO TUESDAY, MAR 1ST 2005,
PIER 90, BOOTH 622, NEW YORK CITY

Swimming, fishing, sailing, hiking,
shopping, cooking, dancing...
We can hardly keep up with grandma!
But anyway, holidays are always
too short.

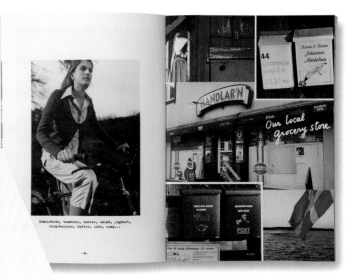

Donaldson
©THE WALT DISNEY COMPANY

The house on the 1001 lakes
a story by Donaldson
spring-summer 2004

FLORE VAN RYN
**Donaldson /
Fashion Catalog**

052

Art Director:
Flore Van Ryn
Designer:
Flore Van Ryn
Client:
Donaldson
Software:
Adobe InDesign
Paper/Materials:
Munken Lynx 300 gsm
(cover), 150 gsm (text)

while the boys
take it easy...

Daydreamin'
on the terrace

THERE

St. Margaret's Residential

053

Art Director:
There
Designer:
There
Client:
Colliers International
Software:
Adobe InDesign,
Adobe Illustrator,
Adobe Photoshop
Paper/Materials:
Uncoated and coated
paper stocks

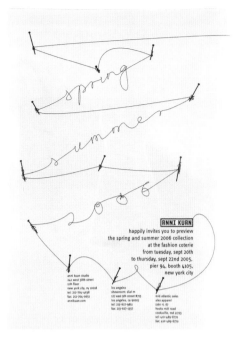

SAGMEISTER INC.
Anni Kuan
Brochure, Pins

054

Art Director:
Stefan Sagmeister
Designer:
Richard The
Client:
Anni Kuan
Software:
Adobe CS
Paper/Materials:
Newsprint

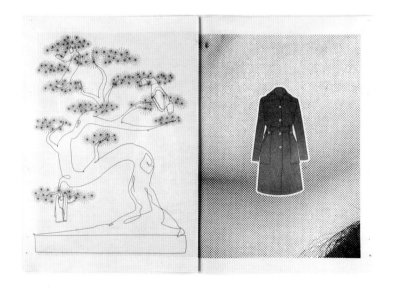

Herman Miller begins thinking about learning spaces by asking a few questions.

What do students and faculty need to learn and teach?

What stimulates intellectual and social growth?

How can a spirit of life-long learning be nurtured?

At Herman Miller, our research-based, problem-solving approach to design directs how we find answers to these questions. Researching human factors, societal change, economic conditions, technology, and environmental sustainability keeps us continually poised to improve our products and their applications, and to better address the needs of our education customers.

The changes we're seeing on campuses create both

ADAPTABLE

BBK STUDIO
Spaces to Learn

055

Art Director:
Sharon Oleniczak
Designer:
Brian Hauch
Client:
Herman Miller
Software:
Adobe Illustrator,
QuarkXPress

Create great places to teach, learn, and grow.

The kinds of spaces you create throughout your campus will make a difference. They have the power to influence culture, attitude, and the effectiveness of faculty and students. They can enhance and support teaching and learning. They can attract students and faculty and reflect a college's spirit and image.

SPACE TO LEARN

Creating Great Places to Teach, Learn, and Grow

HermanMiller

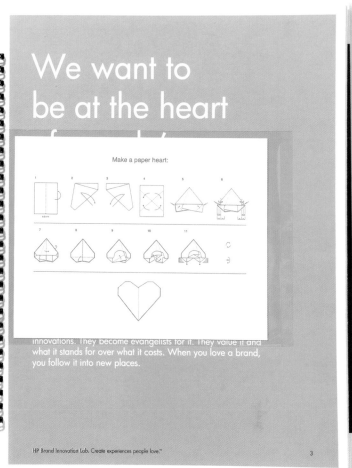

We want to
be at the heart

Make a paper heart:

innovations. They become evangelists for it. They value it and what it stands for over what it costs. When you love a brand, you follow it into new places.

HP Brand Innovation Lab. Create experiences people love.™

3

INSPIRE HEARTS
SPARK COLLABORATION
OPEN MARKETS
UNDERSTAND LIVES
PROVOKE IDEAS
FIND OPPORTUNITIES
SHIFT THINKING
EXPLORE POSSIBILITIES
SHARE KNOWLEDGE
INNOVATE EXPERIENCES
FUEL GROWTH

To build a brand th
we must first build a b

We're working to create a company of people whose p
customers forges a sense of community, fosters morale and sp
innovation and collaboration.

To that end, we bring people together from across our company to share ideas and to foster new ways of thinking and working. We lead workshops where teams collaborate to innovate experiences. We bring in compelling thought leaders for talks and workshops. We take groups on field trips to learn from some of the most-loved brands and most compelling brand experiences in the world. We create a virtual community where people can participate in our journey. And we share what we hear, read and learn so that together we can build a brand experience that creates love.

HP Brand Innovation Lab. Create experience people love.™   13

MIRIELLO
GRAFICO INC.
**Hewlett Packard
Brand Innovation**

056

Designer:
Dennis Garcia
Client:
Hewlett Packard
Software:
Adobe Illustrator
Paper/Materials:
Carnival 80 lb text

300MILLION
**Advocate Paper
Works**

057

Art Director:
Nigel Davies
Designer:
Natalie Turner
Client:
Tullis Russell
Software:
QuarkXPress, OSX
Paper/Materials:
Advocate

Construction at Cardinal Place is well on the way to meeting its autumn opening: the first retail outlets are hoping to be in from September onwards. In fact the last things to take their place will probably be the art, most likely in November.

Meanwhile the artists are in the process of fine-tuning their designs and ensuring everything is correctly rendered when it comes to building them for real. The process of viewing and discussing models and samples with those who will physically carry out the making of their pieces can be painstaking and exacting – but definitely worth the effort.

In this section we talk to each of the artists to find out how their ideas have fared since their initial conceptions, how they have altered in development, and how, if at all, the role of the pieces as public art has affected their final realisation.

TOGETHER DESIGN
**Land Securities
Gallery Art
Newsletter**
058

Designers:
Heidi Lightfoot,
Katja Thielen
Client:
Land Securities
Software:
Adobe InDesign

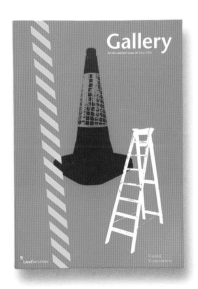

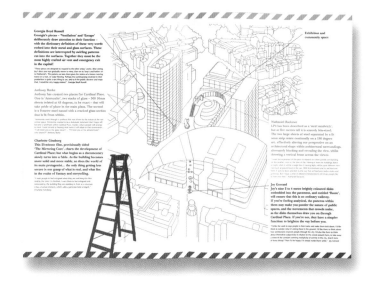

Art Directors:
Ben Graham,
Steve Watson
Designers:
Ben Graham,
Steve Watson
Client:
Teague
Software:
Adobe Illustrator,
Adobe InDesign,
Adobe Photoshop
Paper/Materials:
Luna matte coated
paper, Polystyrene
carton

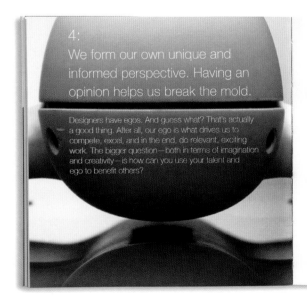

4:
We form our own unique and informed perspective. Having an opinion helps us break the mold.

Designers have egos. And guess what? That's actually a good thing. After all, our ego is what drives us to compete, excel, and in the end, do relevant, exciting work. The bigger question—both in terms of imagination and creativity—is how can you use your talent and ego to benefit others?

27

07
Client: Terabeam
Title: Window Attenuation Meter (WAM)
Terabeam products deliver high bandwidth data via laser technology. Teague developed a friendly and approachable design language to alleviate market anxieties about the safety of laser technology.

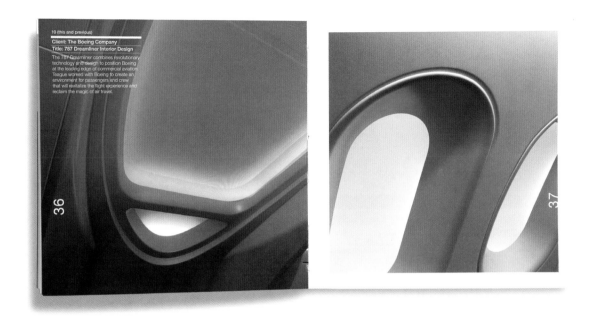

VIVA DOLAN
COMMUNICATIONS
& DESIGN INC.
**Greenville Visitors
Guide**
060

Art Director:
Frank Viva
Designer:
Todd Temporate
Client:
Greenville Convention
& Visitors Bureau
Software:
QuarkXPress
Paper/Materials:
Finch Bright White
Opaque Vellum
70 lb (text), plus 65 lb
(cover)

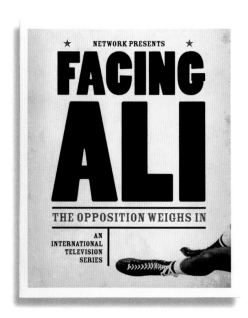

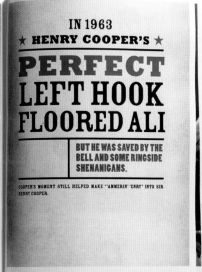

SUBPLOT
DESIGN INC.
Facing Ali

061

Art Directors:
Roy White,
Matthew Clarke
Designer:
Roy White
Client:
Network
Productions Inc.
Paper/Materials:
Pegasus

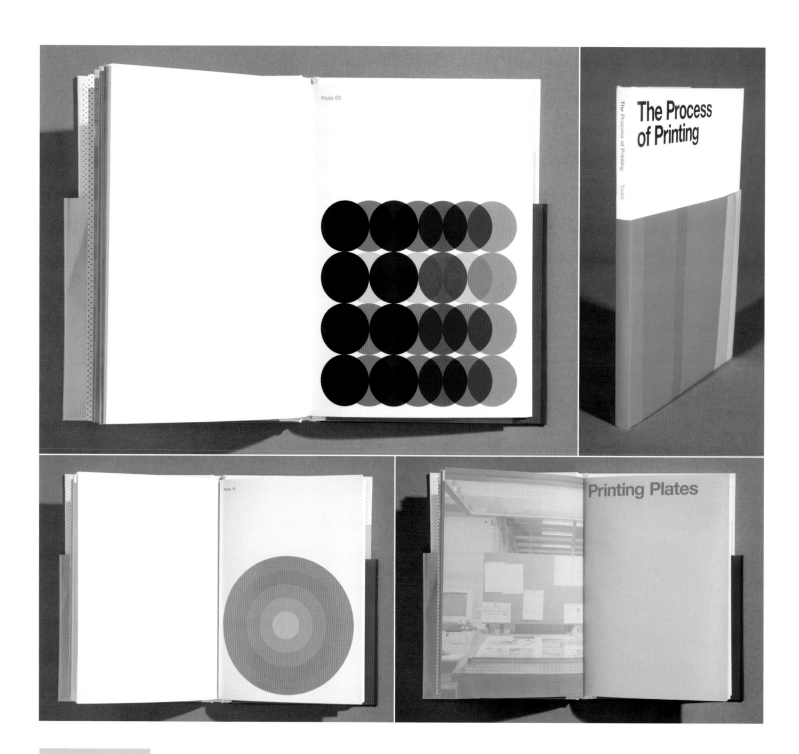

DESIGN PROJECT
**The Process of
Printing**

062

Art Directors:
Andy Probert,
James Littlewood
Designers:
Andy Probert,
James Littlewood

Client:
Team
Software:
QuarkXPress,
Freehand
Paper/Materials:
Hello Silk, Parilux
Matt, Kaskad Osprey
White, Kasdad
Leafbird Green
(Robert Horne)

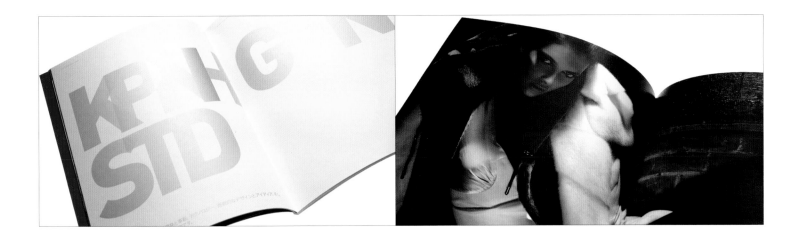

RE-PUBLIC
Kopenhagen Fur
Brandbook

063

Art Director:
Emil Hartvig
Designer:
Emil Hartvig
Client:
Kopenhagen Fur
Software:
Adobe InDesign
Paper/Materials:
200 gsm gloss

Art Director:
Mark Murphy
Client:
Picture Mechanics
Software:
Adobe Photoshop,
QuarkXPress
Paper/Materials:
Five over 5 color
printing

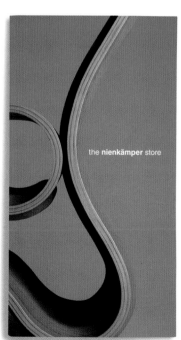

BLOK DESIGN
Nienkamper
Brochure

065

Art Director:
Vanessa Eckstein
Designer:
Vanessa Eckstein
Client:
Nienkamper
Paper|Materials:
Beckett Expression
130 lb

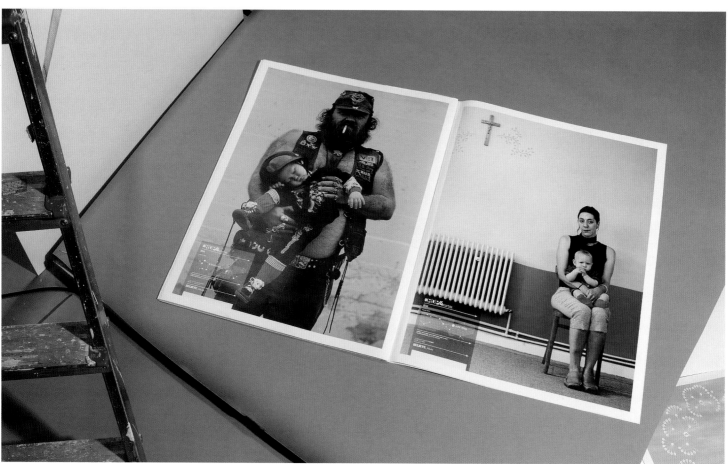

SEGURA INC.
Crop (Large Size Brochure)

066

Art Director:
Carlos Segura
Designers:
Carlos Segura,
Dave Weik,
Chris May,
Tnop
Client:
Corbis
Software:
Adobe InDesign,
Adobe Photoshop,
Adobe Illustrator

DESIGN PROJECT
**Unusual Printing
Surfaces**

067

Art Directors:
Andy Probert,
James Littlewood
Designers:
Andy Probert,
James Littlewood
Client:
ARJO Wiggins
Software:
QuarkXPress,
Freehand
Paper/Materials:
Translucents, Parti-
cles, Metallics, Touch,
Plastics (all from the
Curious Collection
[ARJO Wiggins])

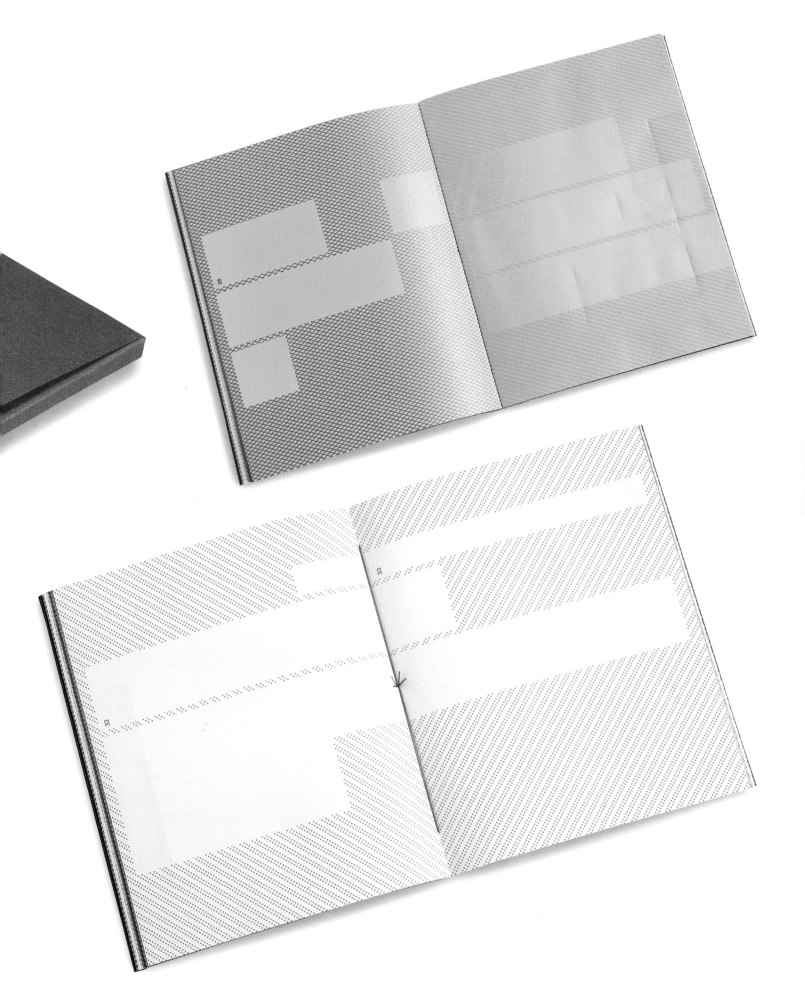

INTENTO 1. VARIAS PIEZAS, VARIAS CONFIGURACIONES

ALGUNAS FORMAS QUE SE PUEDEN MEZCLAR

UNA VAJILLA CON ESPACIOS QUE SE INTEGRAN

DISPONIBLE EN: SAL, CIELO, MUSGO, CHOCOLATE Y ARENA

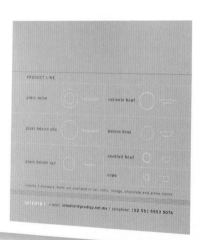

WHAT HAPPENS WHEN CULTURES MINGLE?

NEW WAYS OF INTERACTING BECOME POSSIBLE. NEW WAYS OF COMING TOGETHER DEVELOP. NEW FORMS EVOLVE. AND A NEW WHOLE EMERGES THAT IS MORE THAN THE SUM OF ITS PARTS. THE SPIRIT OF INTENTO IS THE SPIRIT OF COLLABORATION, BETWEEN PLACES, CULTURES AND POINTS OF VIEW. INTENTO 1 IS THE FIRST COLLABORATION, BETWEEN A DESIGNER IN MEXICO AND A DESIGNER IN TORONTO. INTENTO 1 IS A LINE OF REMARKABLE DISHWARE.

WHITE ON WHITE IS FINE. BUT IN YOUR LIFE THERE'S ROOM FOR MORE ROOM FOR SOMETHING A LITTLE MORE SENSUAL. ROOM TO WELCOME ENJOYMENT AND EXPERIENCE. ROOM TO INVITE FREEDOM AND MOVEMENT INTO YOUR HOME. INTENTO 1 IS MADE TO MIX AND MATCH. CREATE ANY CONFIGURATION YOU LIKE.

PRODUCT LINE

plato salsa — caliente bowl

plato básico x6o — básico bowl

plaza básico xgo — cocktail bowl

— ropa

INTENTO 1 e-mail intento@prodigy.net.mx / telephone: [52 55] 5553 5076

INTENTØ 1

INSPIRED TO INTERACT

BLOK DESIGN
Intento 1

068

Art Director:
Vanessa Eckstein
Designers:
Vanessa Eckstein,
Mariana Contegni
Client:
Blok Design
Software:
Adobe Illustrator CS
Paper/Materials:
Starwhite, Sirus
Smooth, 130 lb (Fox
River)

A LANDMARK CONCEPT
WITHOUT EQUAL,
A PRIME INVESTMENT
OPPORTUNITY
WITHOUT RIVAL

On the eastern end of the unspoiled island of Sentosa, located just off the southern coast of the thriving city-state of Singapore, within a stone's throw of the bustling central business district, an extraordinary residential enclave is in the midst of emerging.

Showcasing a unique concept that blends residential, commercial and marina facilities in the form of an integrated waterfront resort, Sentosa Cove introduces a truly magnificent oceanfront lifestyle and community without any equal in the region. Complete with its own fascinating Marina Village, the charming development stands in sharp contrast to the hustle and bustle of cosmopolitan, urban Singapore.

Art Directors:
Leng Soh, Pann Lim,
Roy Poh
Designers:
Leng Soh, Pann Lim,
Roy Poh
Client:
Hobee Group
Software:
Freehand,
Adobe Photoshop
Paper|Materials:
Matte art paper, card,
board

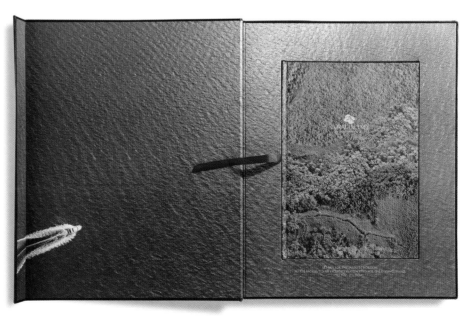

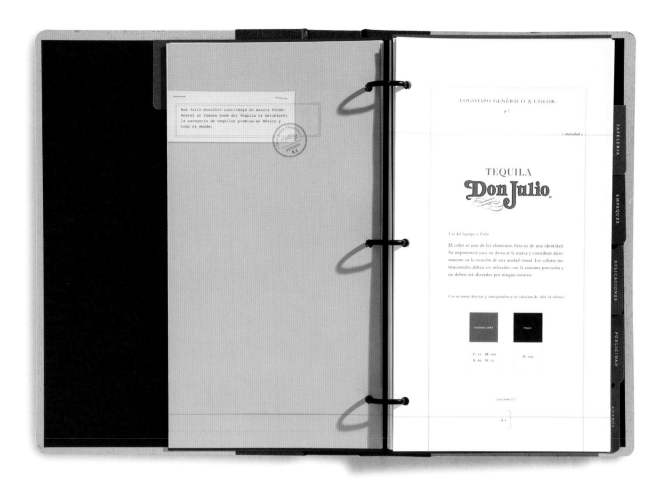

BLOK DESIGN
Don Julio

070

Art Director:
Vanessa Eckstein
Designers:
Vanessa Eckstein,
Vanesa Enriquez,
Mariana Contegni
Client:
Jose Cuervo
Software:
Adobe Illustrator
Paper/Materials:
Sundance Smoke and
Ultrawhite Smooth
(Fox River)

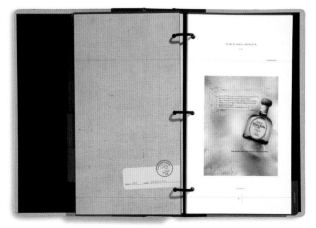

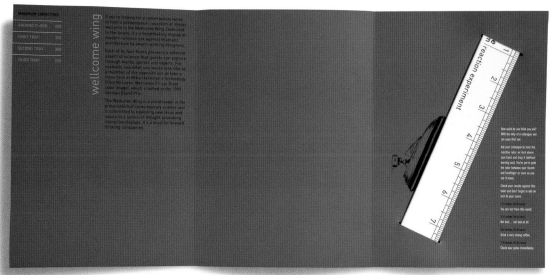

TAXI STUDIO LTD
Serious on the Outside...

071

Art Directors:
Ryan Wills,
Spencer Buck
Designers:
Alex Bane, Karl Wills,
Luke Manning,
Olly Guise
Client:
Science Museum
Software:
QuarkXPress,
Adobe Photoshop,
Adobe Illustrator
Paper/Materials:
Gardapat 13 150 gsm

TAXI STUDIO LTD
**Originals
Brochures**

072

Art Director:
Ryan Wills
Designers:
Olly Guise,
Spencer Buck
Client:
Clarks
Software:
QuarkXPress

STILRADAR

**The Grip
Quadrants**

073

Art Directors:
Raphael Pohland,
Simone Winter
Designers:
Raphael Pohland,
Simone Winter
Client:
Grip AG - Technische
Textilkollktionen
Software:
Freehand
Paper/Materials:
Conqueror 160 gsm,
250 gsm

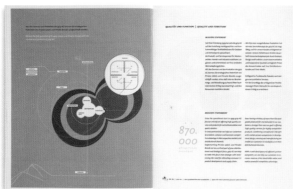

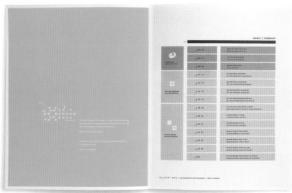

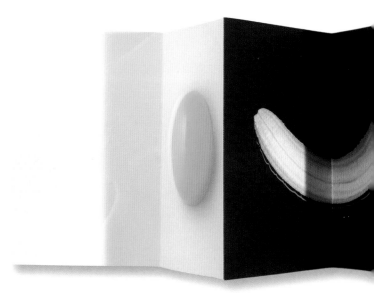

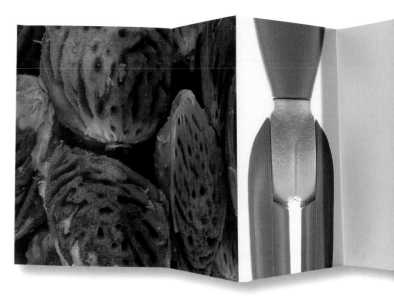

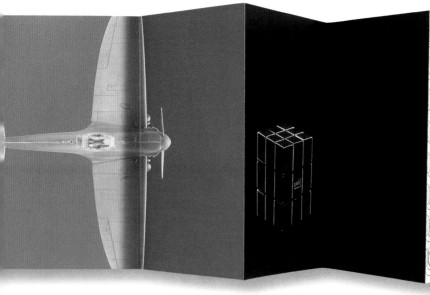

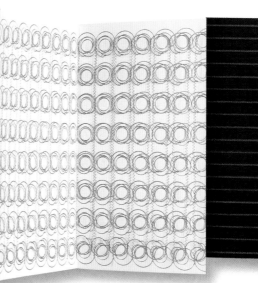

Art Directors:
Nigel Davies,
Dom Bailey,
Martin Lawless
Client:
Tullis Russell
Software:
QuarkXPress, OSX
Paper/Materials:
Naturalis

BRUNAZZI
& ASSOCIATI
**Brochures for
Burgo Papers**
075

Art Director:
Andrea Brunazzi
Designer:
Matteo Marucco
Client:
Cartiere Burgo
Software:
QuarkXPress,
Freehand
Paper/Materials:
Paper and cardboard

ALOOF DESIGN
Georgina Goodman Spring/ Summer

076

Art Director:
Sam Aloof
Designer:
Andrew Scrase
Client:
Georgina Goodman
Software:
Adobe Illustrator,
Adobe Photoshop
Paper/Materials:
Colorplan
& Zen GF Smith

The people are really nice here.

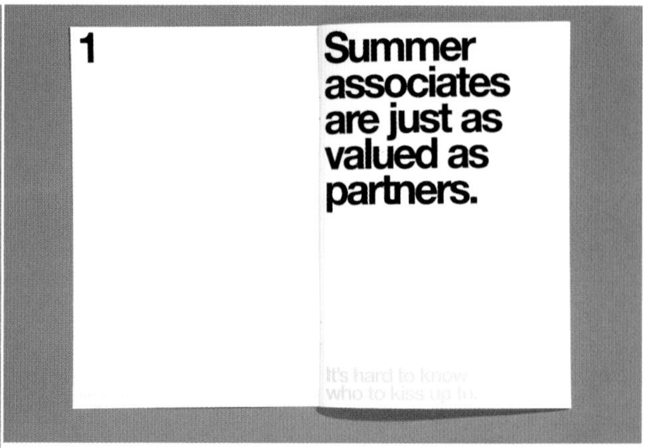

And other nasty rumors about us.

1 Summer associates are just as valued as partners.

It's hard to know who to kiss up to.

CAHAN & ASSOCIATES
Pillsbury Winthrop Rumors Brochure
077

Art Director:
Bill Cahan,
Michael Braley
Designer:
Michael Braley
Client:
Pillsbury Winthrop
Shaw Pittman

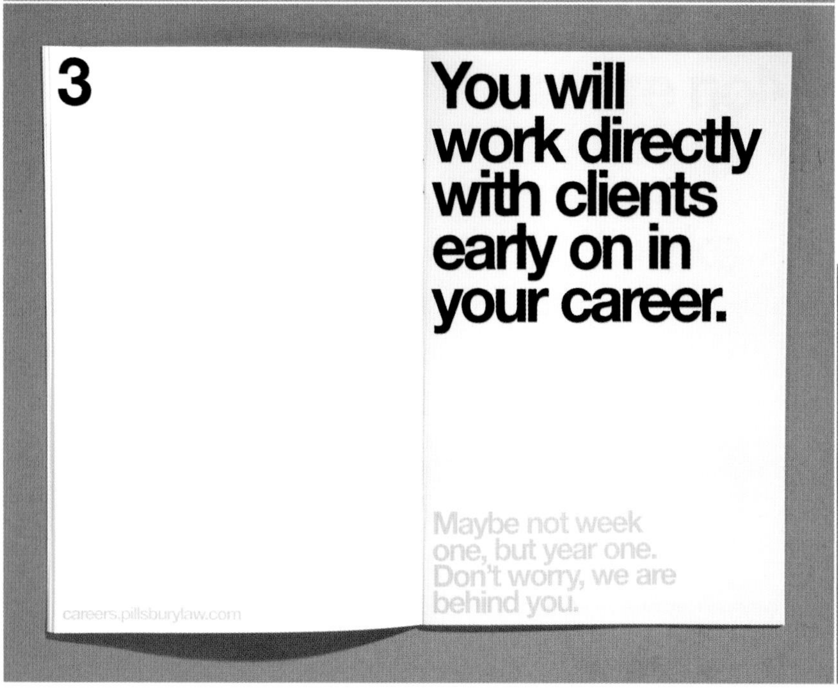

3 You will work directly with clients early on in your career.

Maybe not week one, but year one. Don't worry, we are behind you.

careers.pillsburylaw.com

2 Summer associates are included in real deals.

careers.pillsburylaw.com

It isn't all filet mignon and box seats.

A wealth of opportunity
Retail in The Heart of Walton-on-Thames

THE HEART IS ANTICIPATED TO GENERATE SALES OF ALMOST £50M — MORE THAN HALF THE TOWN CENTRE TOTAL.

THIS TOTAL WILL BE DRIVEN BY AN INCREASE OF 27% IN THE NON-FOOD SPENDING POTENTIAL OF WALTON'S CATCHMENT TO £799M.

BY 2009 TOTAL RETAIL SALES FOR WALTON ARE SET TO MORE THAN DOUBLE TO £91M.

THIS BREAKS DOWN AS:

CLOTHING/ FOOTWEAR	£31M
PERSONAL GOODS	£24M
HOUSEHOLD GOODS	£16M
LEISURE GOODS	£20M

ICO DESIGN
CONSULTANCY
**Shopping Mall
in Walton**

078

Art Directors:
Andy Spencer,
Vivek Bhatia
Designer:
Andy Spencer
Client:
O+H Properties LTD
Software:
Adobe InDesign
Paper/Materials:
Mega Matt

The untapped market

Walton-on-Thames has a 154,000-strong catchment population.

It sits within Elmbridge, the second-most propserous community in the country and one of the largest and fastest-growing boroughs.

Populated by discerning consumers who love to shop, spending on non-foods is £3,648 per capita, nearly 50% higher than the national average.

Introduction

The Heart is a brand new mixed-use development which will transform the town centre of Walton-on-Thames, an area with one of the most affluent populations in the country.

By creating a new heart for the local community, it will make the town centre an attractive place in which to live and shop.

With an innovative mix of multiple and independent retailers, The Heart will give Walton-on-Thames a real point of difference over neighbouring towns.

Rock Galpin
Designers Guild

2 seater sofa and chaise longue in L shaped configuration
upholstered furniture
system comprises 2 and 3 seater sofa, chaise longue (2 sizes),
easy chair

Afroditi Krassa
John Lewis

Candy light
blown glass, metal and light fitting

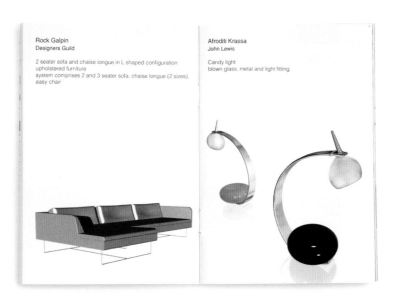

ALOOF DESIGN
Eureka 2005
Brochure

079

Art Director:
Sam Aloof
Designer:
Andrew Scrase
Client:
Design Nation
Software:
Adobe Illustrator

Beatriz Matud
Heal's

Koi home/office computer work trolley
powder-coated steel tubing and sheet metal

Helen Yardley
Heal's

Dash hand-tufted rug
100% wool, art silk hand-tufting
collection comprises Dash, Eclipse, Eureka

Art Director:
Nessim Higson
Designer:
Nessim Higson
Client:
Lion Gate Films
Software:
Adobe Photoshop,
Adobe Illustrator

CAHAN
& ASSOCIATES
**See: The Potential
of Place, 2nd Issue**

082

Art Directors:
Bill Cahan,
Todd Richards,
Steve Frykholm
Designers:
Todd Richards,
Nicholas Davison
Client:
Herman Miller
Paper/Materials:
International Papers
Via Recycled

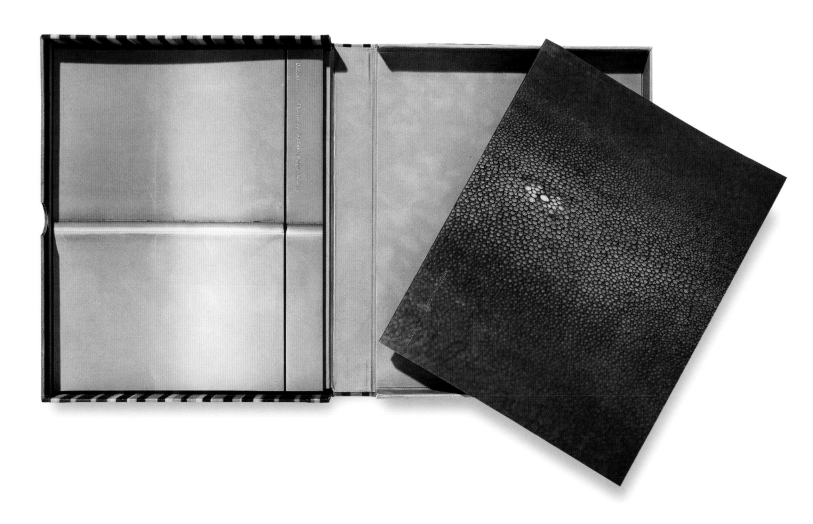

Master Bedroom   This spacious yet comfortable room leads off to two bathrooms, each designed with its own character, vast wardrobe spaces, and a gentlemen's club-style study.

ICO DESIGN
CONSULTANCY
**Freehold Property
Brochure**
083

Art Director:
Vivek Bhatia
Designer:
Vivek Bhatia
Client:
Bath + Bath
Software:
Adobe InDesign,
Adobe Photoshop
Paper/Materials:
Naturalis, Curious
(main brochure),
Redeem, Curious
(plans book),
Flockage (box)

SEA
Staverton
Brochure

084

Art Director:
Bryan Edmondson
Designer:
Stuart L Bailey
Client:
Staverton
Software:
QuarkXPress,
Adobe Photoshop
Paper/Materials:
PVC (cover),
Paralux (text)

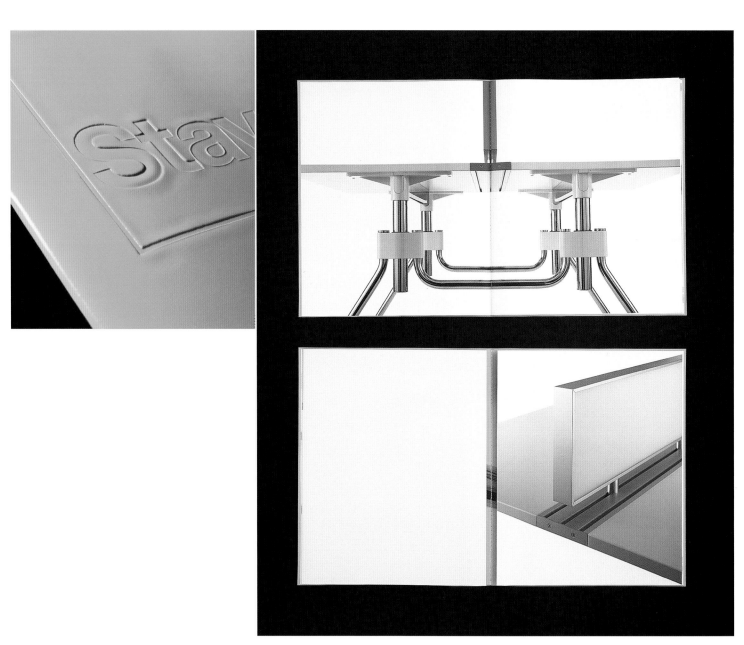

PAST, PRESENT & FUTURE

DOWLING DESIGN
& ART DIRECTION
**Promotional
Booklet**

085

Art Director:
John Dowling
Designer:
John Dowling
Client:
Future Designs
Software:
QuarkXPress
Paper/Materials:
Neptune Unique
(Fenner), Colorplan
Ebony (GF Smith)

When we think of history, we think about the debt we owe to the inventor of the light bulb, Thomas Alva Edison.

A true pioneer, Edison gave us many inventions, including the phonograph, the kinescope, centralised power systems (electricity generators) and, of course, the light bulb... or did he?

In 1809, Humphry Davy, an English chemist, invented the first electric light. 26 years later, James Bowman Lindsey used a prototype light bulb to demonstrate his constant electric lighting system.

Henricg Globel, a German watchmaker, invented the first true light bulb in 1854, with a carbonised bamboo filament in a glass bulb. In 1875, Henry Woodward and Matthew Evans patented a light bulb design.

Who knows what the future may bring? You can rest assured that here at FUTURE Designs, we'll be keeping abreast of any further developments, and will continue to innovate in our own field, like Davy, Globel, and Edison before us.

With exceptional engineering and innovative yet appropriate lighting solutions... the future is light.

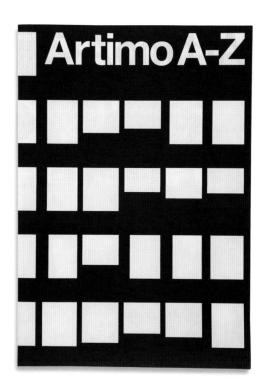

Art Director:
Experimental Jetset
Designer:
Experimental Jetset
Client:
Artimo

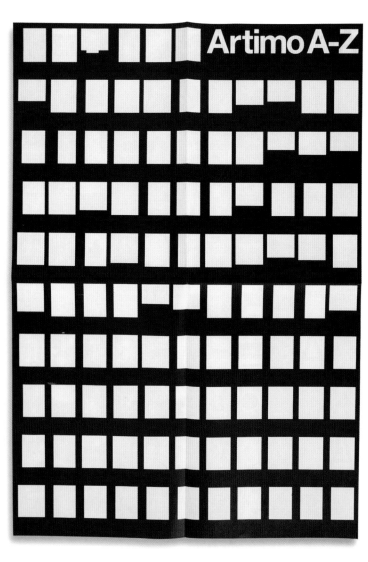

ATELIER WORKS
Cut Book (three books in one for a film animator)
087

Art Director:
Quentin Newark
Designer:
D. Hawkins
Client:
G.F. Smith
Software:
Adobe Photoshop,
QuarkXPress

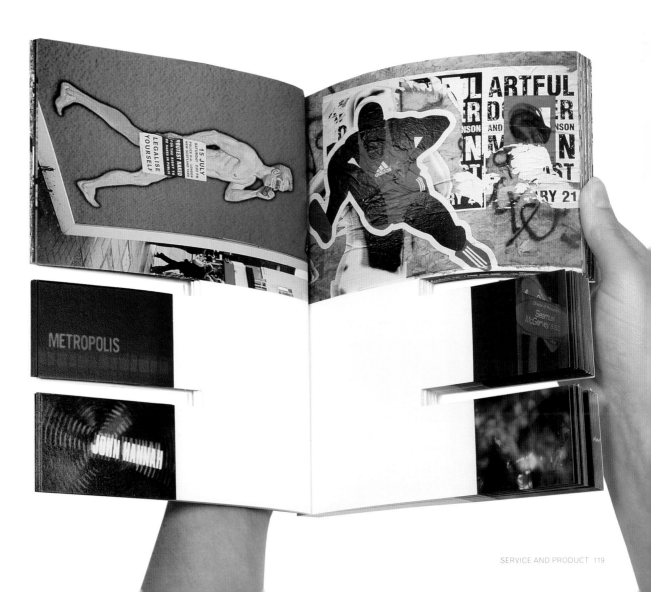

Art Director:
Andy Spencer
Designer:
Andy Spencer
Client:
Hammerson
Software:
Adobe InDesign
Paper/Materials:
Naturalis

10 – 11
Park Lane's most
prestigious address

**100 Park Lane is rich in
architectural heritage.**

In 1827, John William Ward,
son of William Ward, Viscount
Dudley and Ward, commissioned
the architect William Atkinson
to design and build the first
Dudley home on this site.

The original Dudley House
picture gallery, shown here
in its former glory

Mayfair's superb location
is popular with the capital's
discerning residents and
visitors alike.

100 Park Lane is surrounded
by neighbours of the highest
calibre, from international
corporations to five-star hotels,
and the best in fine dining,
entertainment and luxury retail.

Many original Regency and
Early Victorian interior details
remain, adding to 100 Park
Lane's character.

Some of the building's existing
art work – including some fine
work by Joshua Reynolds –
is also available.

Portraits of
Viscount Dudley
and Lady Ward
hang on the
main staircase

Art Director:
Kit Hinrichs
Designer:
Takayo Muroga
Client:
Sappi Fine Papers
Software:
Adobe InDesign
Paper/Materials:
Sappi McCoy

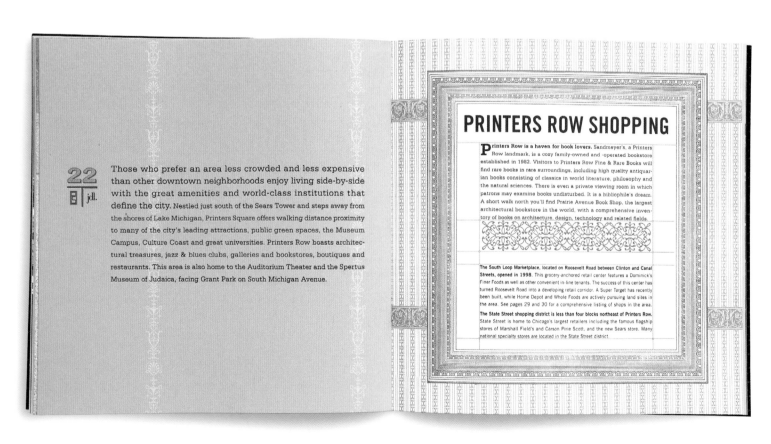

Art Director:
Dawn Hancock
Designers:
Dawn Hancock,
Aaron Shimer,
Antonio Garcia
Client:
JDL Development Corp.
Software:
Adobe Photoshop,
Adobe Illustrator,
Adobe InDesign
Paper/Materials:
New Leaf
Reincarnation Matte

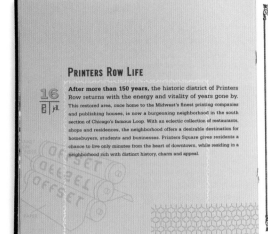

Printers Row Life

After more than 150 years, the historic district of Printers Row returns with the energy and vitality of years gone by. This restored area, once home to the Midwest's finest printing companies and publishing houses, is now a burgeoning neighborhood in the south section of Chicago's famous Loop. With an eclectic collection of restaurants, shops and residences, the neighborhood offers a desirable destination for homebuyers, students and businesses. Printers Square gives residents a chance to live only minutes from the heart of downtown, while residing in a neighborhood rich with distinct history, charm and appeal.

Considered part of the South Loop, Printers Row is an area just south of the Loop (Chicago's downtown) with its distinctive housing composed of condominiums and loft apartments created out of former warehouses, printing plants and other historic buildings.

PRINTERS ROW

NORTH BOUNDARY: 500 S CONGRESS
SOUTH BOUNDARY: 800 S POLK
EAST BOUNDARY: 0 E/W STATE
WEST BOUNDARY: 100 W CLARK
SUB-NEIGHBORHOOD OF: SOUTH LOOP
41°53'N, 87°38'W

TABLE OF CONTENTS

PRINTERS ROW SYNOPSIS

D **URING THE DAY,** the neighborhood is an easy walk to offices in the Loop, off Michigan Avenue, or the LaSalle Street financial centers. After hours, the district is alive with anything from restaurants, pubs, and blues clubs to coffee shops and bookstores.

It boasts famous blues clubs, eclectic music venues and neighborhood taverns. Its annual book fair, the Chicago Tribune Printers Row Book Fair, gathers authors, poets, speakers and, of course, a great selection of books.

Printers Row is also walking distance to the Spertus Museum of Judaica, the newly reconstructed Soldier Field and Chicago's Museum Campus, with the Field Museum, Adler Planetarium and Shedd Aquarium just blocks away.

Enjoy the excitement of downtown with the serenity of a century old historic district. Printers Square, located at the heart of Printers Row, is just minutes from Grant Park, Millennium Park, shopping on State Street, Chicago's famous Theater District, the "L", Metra, and South Shore Line stations, Sears Tower, US Cellular Field, Burnham Harbor and beautiful Lake Michigan, Harold Washington Library, Dearborn Park, five-star restaurants, world class

PRESS Nº 2

A COMPLETE TWO-REVOLUTION PRINTING PRESS UNIT

ATELIER WORKS
**Made in UK
(Promotion for
Product Designers)**

091

Art Director:
John Powner
Designer:
A. Browne
Client:
Factory Design
Software:
Adobe Photoshop,
QuarkXPress

Portfolio No. 036

Since the beginning of consumerism, the humble tin has been one of the most enduring forms of product design.

A simple, robust method of preserving food, the tin became a brilliant way of advertising and presenting goods and, thanks to Warhol's soup cans, a consumer icon in itself.

We saw a parallel between the tin and our own ambitions; applying simple and robust design solutions to our work, thereby brilliantly influencing consumer culture ourselves.

Light Projects

Appropriate design means appropriate solutions. Even when a product is not intended as the main focus of attention, considered detail, functional benefits and reduced costs all combine to highlight how design can be used as a strategic business tool.

The Royal Academy is a demanding place to illuminate. Functionally and aesthetically, the demands are high on luminaires to work within such an historic and busy environment. They must be unobtrusive and effective.

The public must appreciate what they achieve, yet not notice them, and the lighting designers must be able to use them in a pressurised working environment to create the varied effects they require.

The RA range by Light Projects for the Royal Academy is the result of close liaison between manufacturer, lighting designer, architect and Factory – the product designers.

By integrating the newly developed transformer into the lamp body, Light Projects were establishing a major breakthrough in the technology used in track mounted exhibition lighting and rightly realised the need to develop the technical package into a product suitable for the Royal Academy.

The product needed to integrate with the new trackway being installed and had to provide the exhibition lighting designers with the flexibility required to create the visual and lighting effects to illuminate high profile exhibitions.

After various consultations with all parties a series of concepts were presented by Factory.

Major issues had been identified – no tools to be used in adjustment so you don't drop a spanner on a Rodin! – the need for rapid and yet finely tuned adjustment – and the easy addition of a multitude of specialised attachments.

The final product – the result of extensive consultation and using the preferred manufacturing method of die casting – is a pleasing blend of technical and ergonomic requirements which have been combined to create a slim, adaptable and streamlined product that sits comfortably within any environment, helping the lighting designer to do his work efficiently and creatively.

LIEBLING /
WORDS

HAB' GEFUNDEN!

Weich

nuit de noces

LIEBLING /
SPECIMEN

» 07

CHARACTERS

A B C D E F G H I J K L M N O P
Q R S T U V W X Y Z Ä Á Â Ã
Ç É È Ê Ö Ó Ò Ô Ü Ú Ù Û Í Ì Î Ï Ø
a b c d e f g h i j k l m n o p
q r s t u v w x y z ß ä ö ü ø

FIGURES & FORMS

1 2 3 4 5 6 7 8 9 0 € ¢ $ £ ¥
1 2 3 4 5 6 7 8 9 0 & & § #
® © @ % ‰ ™ * + - = ∞

NINA DAVID
KOMMUNIKA-
TIONSDESIGN
Font Report

092

Art Director:
Nina David
Designer:
Nina David
Client:
Font-o-Rama
Software:
QuarkXPress,
Adobe Photoshop,
Adobe Illustrator
Paper/Materials:
Splendorgel

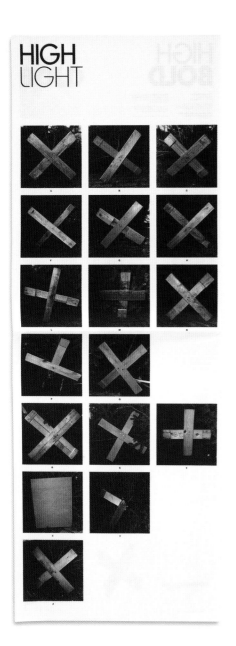

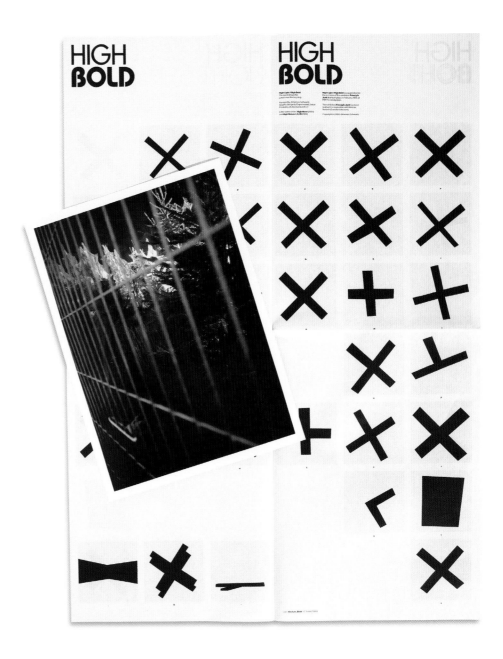

EXPERIMENTAL
JETSET
**High Light /
High Bold**

093

Art Director:
Experimental Jetset
Designer:
Experimental Jetset
Client:
Johannes Schwartz

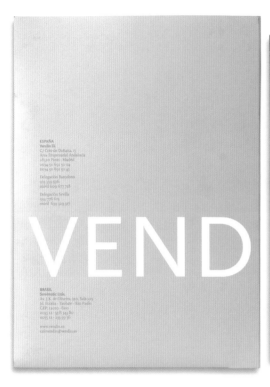

LSD
Corporate
Brochure

094

Art Director:
Gabriel Martínez
Designers:
Gabriel Martínez,
Paz Martín
Client:
Vendin
Software:
Adobe Photoshop,
Freehand
Paper/Materials:
Offset

Art Director:
Patrick Crowe
Designers:
Dan Behrens,
Sarah Anderson
Client:
Trio Development
Software:
Adobe Illustrator,
Adobe Photoshop
Paper/Materials:
130 lb Cougar Double
Thick Cover

KAMPER BRANDS
**Brochure for
Condominium
Project**

096

Art Director:
Patrick Crowe
Designer:
Sladjana Dirakovi
Client:
The Wall Company
Software:
Adobe Illustrator,
Adobe Photoshop
Paper/Materials:
Domtar Proterra
(Coastal Whites),
cotton bag

RUSSELL
WARREN-FISHER
**Printed Matter
No.1**
097

Art Director:
Russell Warren-Fisher
Designer:
Russell Warren-Fisher
Client:
Ripe/Park Lane
Software:
QuarkXPress,
Adobe InDesign,
Adobe Photoshop
Paper|Materials:
Consort Royal

RUSSELL
WARREN-FISHER
Orangebox
Corporate Brochure
98

Art Director:
Gerry Taylor
Designer:
Russell Warren-Fisher
Client:
Orangebox
Software:
QuarkXPress,
Adobe Photoshop
Paper/Materials:
Consort Royal

I SEE IT AS MORE OF A WORK SURFACE THAN A DESK.

Shopping is more than a simple necessity. As all retailers know, it's more than a trip to stock up with life's essentials. Shopping is a passion. An urge. An urge that can strike anyone at any time, anywhere.

We understand. We're coming to the rescue, bringing new shopping opportunities to Victoria, Bankside, 'Midtown' and the City. These areas will soon have enough shops to satisfy the needs of frustrated shoppers and ambitious retailers.

It's part of our commitment to the capital. It's our Capital Commitment; a programme costing up to £2 billion over seven years. Like our fellow Londoners, we know how to spend. We love shopping too.

Love*Shopping*

NB:STUDIO
**Love Shopping –
New Development**

99

Art Directors:
Nick Finney, Ben Stott, Alan Dye
Designers:
Sarah Fullerton, Martin Morrell
Client:
Land Securities

SEA
Beyon Brochure

100

Art Director:
Bryan Edmondson
Designer:
Stuart L Bailey
Client:
Beyon
Software:
QuarkXPress,
Adobe Photoshop
Paper/Materials:
Construction board
(cover), PhoenixMo-
tion Xenon (text)

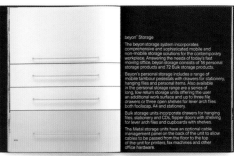

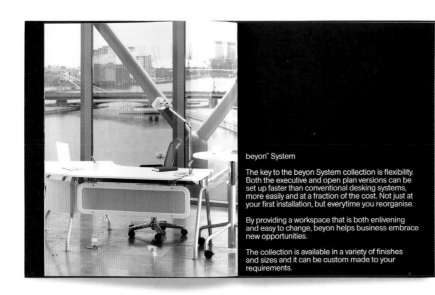

beyon™ System

The key to the beyon System collection is flexibility. Both the executive and open plan versions can be set up faster than conventional desking systems, more easily and at a fraction of the cost. Not just at your first installation, but everytime you reorganise.

By providing a workspace that is both enlivening and easy to change, beyon helps business embrace new opportunities.

The collection is available in a variety of finishes and sizes and it can be custom made to your requirements.

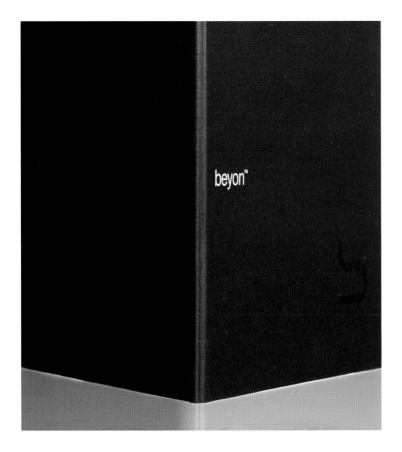

beyon™

beyon™ philosophy

To create working environments which are open and inviting, that inspire and motivate, creating feelings of confidence.

Designing clean and contemporary furniture that captures the essence of the modern with the substance and beauty of the classic.

day

leather lane assumes a multitude of identities during the course of each working day. as dawn breaks you can snap into focus with a workout at one of three nearby health clubs or whatever kind of breakfast you want there is a local establishment to suit. sweeps' location is ideal for quickly getting to work in any of london's central business hubs.

as the day wears on, so the gastronomic options increase. smiths buzzes all day long, and the st john bakery offers both freshly baked bread and an exquisite lunch and supper menu. during weekdays, leather lane is home to the thriving 300 year old lunchtime market.

the area also houses facilities to rival, and often surpass, those of any british high street. mcqueens in st john st, while annie khan in hatton garden is well-regarded in the city. nearby hatton garden, london's jewellery capital, features award-winning designer, shaun leane, who crafts bespoke pieces.

Art Director:
Morag Myerscough
Designer:
Morag Myerscough
Photographer:
Richard Learoyd
Client:
Derwent Valley

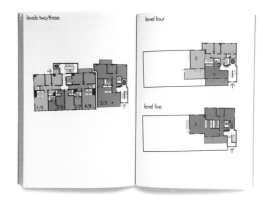

Hull
GF Smith
Lockwood Street
Hull HU2 OHL

Telephone
01482 323 503
Facsimile
01482 223 174
Email
info@gfsmith.com

www.gfsmith.com

London
GF Smith
2 Leathermarket
Weston Street
London SE1 3ET

Telephone
020 7407 6174
Facsimile
020 7403 1037
Email
london@gfsmith.com

Printed on
Monadnock 148 gsm

Produced
12/04

Paper from GF Smith

Paper from GFSmith

White Book

Art Director:
Bryan Edmondson
Designer:
Ryan Jones
Client:
GF Smith
Software:
QuarkXPress,
Adobe Photoshop
Paper/Materials:
Mixed stock

Snow White, wearing maroon,
revealing her yellow streak

Art Director:
John Dowling
Designer:
John Dowling
Photographer:
Steve Rees
Client:
Robert Welch
Software:
QuarkXPress
Paper/Materials:
Millenium Silk (Fenner)

Candlesticks

Robert Welch
Campden Cookware

Double Four Candlestick
Polished stainless steel
cylindrical base with
elevated sconce and
candle support spike
Height 12cm Width 11.2cm
£40.00
4" x 4" Candle, available in
black, white, pink or brown
£8.00

Double Six Candlestick
Polished stainless steel
cylindrical base with
elevated sconce and
candle support spike
Height 17.3cm Width 11.2cm
£46.00
6" x 6" Candle, available in
black, white, pink or brown
£10.00

Hobart Candlestick Large
Cast iron design classic from
1962. Available in powder
coated black or green
Height 17.5cm
Base diameter 12cm
£25.00
3" x 6" Ivory candle
£3.25

Candle Snuffers
Mild steel with a brass
ball, polished stainless
steel handle and dish
Available in black or copper
Height 10.3cm Width 8.5cm
£18.00

Long Candle Snuffer
Mild steel with a brass ball
Available in black only
Length 37.3cm **£16.00**

Robert Welch
Campden Cookware
The Robert Welch Campden
Cookware is constructed
from the finest 18/10 stainless
steel. The base of each pan
features a copper/stainless
steel 3 ply sandwich, allowing
for even heat distribution
across the whole base and
leaving no hot spots.

Certain pan interiors® are
coated with Excalibur®,
the patented reinforced
non-stick system, which
requires less oil/fat for frying
so creating healthier cooking.
(*See individual pan text).

Robert Welch Campden
Cookware is suitable for all
cooking methods, including
Induction cooking.

Conferences and Meetings

Conference rooms at the Wallace Collection are available for hire Monday to Friday, ideal for private functions.

Lecture Theatre
9am–5pm
2 hour session
100 people
Wheelchair Capacity 2

Meeting Room
9am–5pm
2 hour session
30 people theatre
22 boardroom

This comfortable modern Lecture Theatre is hung with gilded picture frames reminding you that you are in the heart of the Wallace Collection. It is available for day hire.

The 100-seat air-conditioned theatre has a raked floor and is equipped with a screen suitable for front projection. The hire fee includes a PA system, a data/video projector & DVD player. Two 35mm carousel projectors, a flipchart and pens are available on request.

The hire fee includes the use of the Meeting Room for registration and refreshments.

Daytime Catering

Refreshments can be arranged by the Café Bagatelle, the Wallace Collection restaurant franchise. Please contact the Restaurant Manager on 020 7563 9505 for advice, menus and costs.

Next to the Lecture Theatre is the Meeting Room, a beautifully proportioned room with French windows looking on to the Porphyry Court.

Evening Hire

Tailor made packages for evening can be arranged as part of any evening hire of the galleries or sculpture gardens.

All prices quoted are exclusive of VAT and details are correct at the time of going to press.

Corporate Entertaining
At the Wallace Collection

HGV
Wallace Collection Corporate/Wedding Brochure

104

Art Director:
Pierre Vermeir
Designer:
Tommy Taylor
Client:
Wallace Collection
Software:
Adobe Photoshop,
QuarkXPress
Paper/Materials:
Zanders Medley

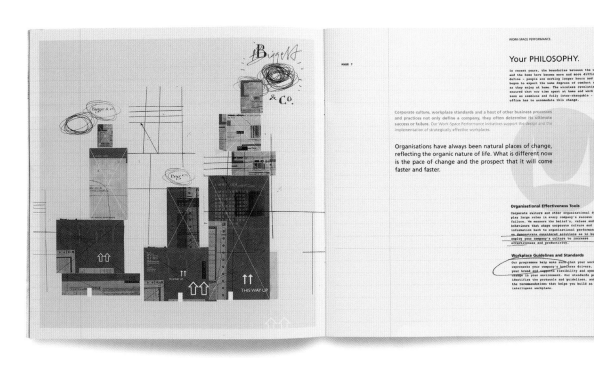

PAGE 7

Your PHILOSOPHY.

In recent years, the boundaries between the workplace and the home have become more and more difficult to define — people are working longer hours and have begun to expect the same degrees of comfort at work as they enjoy at home. The wireless revolution has ensured that our time spent at home and work can be seen as seamless and fully inter-changeable — the office has to accommodate this change.

Corporate culture, workplace standards and a host of other business processes and practices not only define a company, they often determine its ultimate success or failure. Our Work-Space Performance initiatives support the design and the implementation of strategically effective workplaces.

Organisations have always been natural places of change, reflecting the organic nature of life. What is different now is the pace of change and the prospect that it will come faster and faster.

Organisational Effectiveness Tools

Corporate culture and other organisational dynamics play large roles in every company's success or failure. We measure the belief's, values and behaviours that shape corporate culture and tie this information back to organisational performance. Then we demonstrate considered solutions as to how best employ your company's culture to increase effectiveness and productivity.

Workplace Guidelines and Standards

Our programmes help make sure that your workplace represents your company's business drivers, embodies your brand and supports flexibility and speed of change in your environment. Our standards program identifies the protocols and guidelines, and makes the recommendations that helps you build an effective, intelligent workplace.

RUSSELL
WARREN-FISHER
**Workplace Intel-
ligence Brochure**

105

Designer:
Russell Warren-Fisher
Client:
Herman Miller
Software:
QuarkXPress,
Adobe Photoshop
Paper/Materials:
Redeem

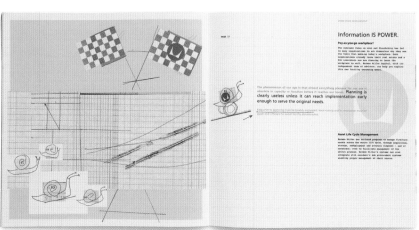

PAGE 17

Information IS POWER.

Pay-as-you-go workplace?

The constant focus on cost and flexibility has led to many organisations to ask themselves why they own the tools that make-up today's workplace. Such organisations already lease their real estate and a few innovators are now choosing to lease the workplace as well. Herman Miller Capital, with its independent team of advisors, can help you explore this new leasing ownership model.

The phenomenon of our age is that almost everything planned for our use is obsolete in capacity or function before it reaches our hands. **Planning is clearly useless unless it can reach implementation early enough to serve the original needs.**

Asset Life Cycle Management

Herman Miller has tailored programs to manage furniture assets across the entire life cycle, through acquisition, storage, redeployment and eventual disposal — and if service ever — to facilitate seamless management of the entire process. Herman Miller's systems can even integrate with customer's own procurement systems enabling proper management of their assets.

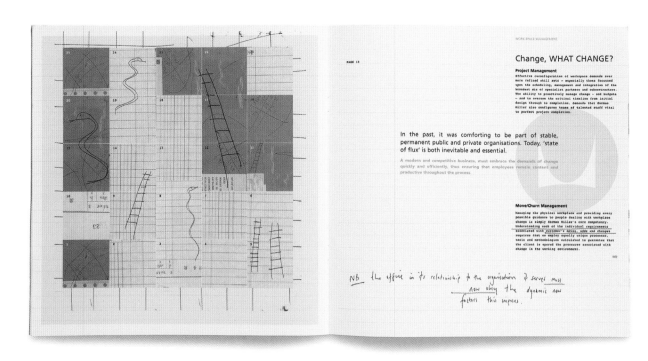

PAGE 15

Change, WHAT CHANGE?

Project Management

Effective reconfiguration of workplaces demands ever more refined skill sets — especially those focussed upon the scheduling, management and integration of the broadest mix of specialist partners and subcontractors. The ability to proactively manage change — and budgets — and to oversee the critical timeline from initial design through to completion, demands that Herman Miller also configures teams of talented staff vital to perfect project completion.

In the past, it was comforting to be part of stable, permanent public and private organisations. Today, 'state of flux' is both inevitable and essential.

A modern and competitive business, must embrace the demands of change quickly and efficiently, thus ensuring that employees remain content and productive throughout the process.

Move/Churn Management

Managing the physical workplace and providing every possible guidance to people dealing with workplace change is simply Herman Miller's core competency. Understanding each of the individual requirements associated with customer's moves, adds and changes requires that we employ equally unique processes, tools and methodologies calculated to guarantee that the client is spared the pressures associated with change in working environments.

NB the office in its relationship to the organisation it serves must now obey the dynamic new factors this imposes.

One Hundred Knightsbridge · London

NB:STUDIO
One Hundred Knightsbridge

106

Art Directors:
Nick Finney, Ben Stott,
Alan Dye
Client:
Land Securities

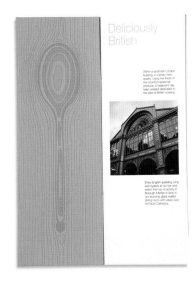

HGV
Roast

107

Art Director:
Pierre Vermeir
Designer:
Pierre Vermeir
Client:
Roast Restaurant
Software:
Adobe Illustrator,
Adobe InDesign
Paper/Materials:
Splendorgel Extra
White (Popset Fawn)

Roast celebrates Britain's food heritage and our farming industry. Classical and modern dishes are prepared with care and precision, using the finest of ingredients – some of which are sourced by the stallholders in the market.

A centrepiece attraction of the restaurant is a large spit oven that may be roasting a suckling pig one day, ribs of beef the next and wild birds on the third.

Seafood and salads with wild and organic leaves will feature strongly on our daily changing menu alongside pies and puddings.

We aim to deliver all of this with charming and efficient service. We look forward to welcoming you.

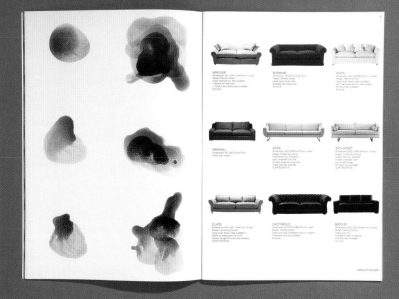

STUDIO
MYERSCOUGH
**Conran Shop
Furniture**
108

Art Director:
Morag Myerscough
Designer:
Morag Myerscough
Photographer:
Richard Learoyd
Client:
Conran Shop,
Polly Dickens
& Terence Conran

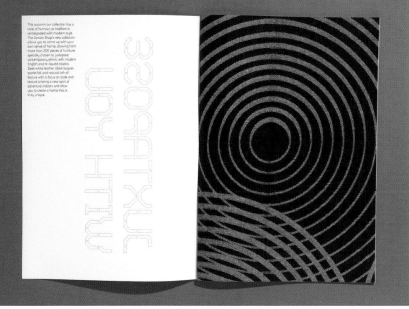

PENTAGRAM
DESIGN, LONDON
Edmund De Waal
Catalogue
109

Art Director:
Angus Hyland
Client:
Blackwell: De Waal

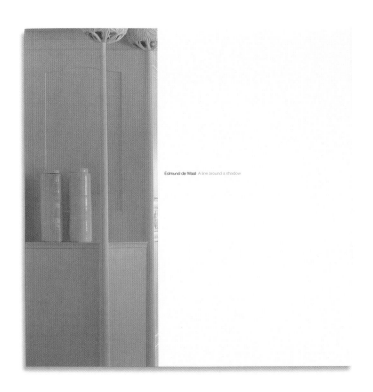

Edmund de Waal A line around a shadow

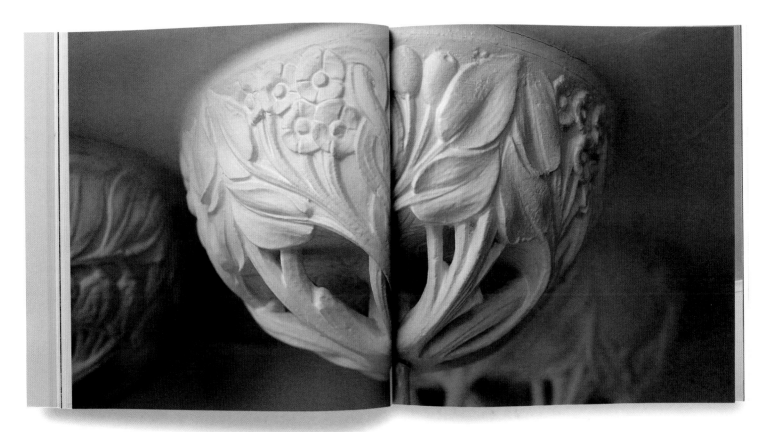

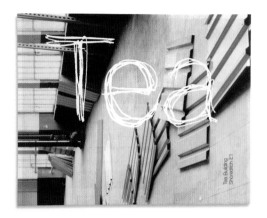

STUDIO
MYERSCOUGH
Tea Building

110

Art Director:
Morag Myerscough
Designers:
Morag Myerscough,
Chris Merrick
Photographer:
Richard Learoyd
Client:
Derwent Valley

The end is nigh. Burn all the books. Words are done for. Pictures are the future. If you believe everything you read, you wouldn't be reading. Books would be doorstops and brochures would be shelved. And as for direct mail and magazines, the less said about them the better. But the truth is different.

ink! is a team of copywriters, journalists and communication strategists who believe words can still have a huge impact. We work with design agencies and businesses offering strategic advice for their literature, writing words that jump off the page and making every letter count. Starting here.

in k!

MYTTON WILLIAMS

Ink! Promotional Brochure

111

Art Director:
Bob Mytton
Designer:
Tracey Bowes
Client:
Ink! Copywriters
Software:
Adobe InDesign
Paper/Materials:
Challenger Offset
120 gsm

Words are a little like icebergs. Beneath the elegant bits on the surface is an unseen force holding everything together. In writing, this is the thought behind the words; the strategy that makes your communication stand out. So before we put pen to paper, we pause for a while.

And take a moment to fully understand your aims and challenges, your company's brand values and tone of voice, your audience's attitudes and behaviour. At these opening stages, our strategic thought can really add value. Then, when everything's in place, we start to write.

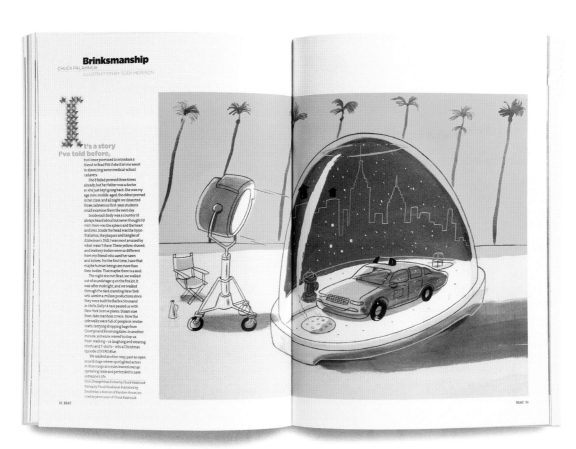

MIKE
LACKERSTEEN
DESIGN
Beat
112

Art Director:
Mike Lackersteen
Designer:
Mike Lackersteen
Client:
Heart
Paper|Materials:
Matrisse Avorio
(cover), Neptune
Unique Fenner Paper
(text)

...of wonder and love

...of sheer luxury and taste

PENTAGRAM
DESIGN, LONDON
**One & Only
Brochure**
113

Art Director:
John Rushworth
Client:
One & Only

...of excitement and discovery

ARTS

NB:STUDIO 114, 118, 148, 149	**CHENG DESIGN** 115, 140	**CARTLIDGE LEVENE** 116	**ROSE** 117
BLUE RIVER 119	**TOMATO KOŠIR S.P.** 120	**BURGEFF DESIGN** 121	**LIPPA PEARCE** 122, 156	**SAGMEISTER INC.** 123	**BBK STUDIO** 124
BILLY BLUE CREATIVE, PRECINCT 125	**BC, MH, JAMES LAMBERT** 126	**VIVA DOLAN COMMUNICA-TIONS & DESIGN INC.** 127	**FANCLUB-PROJECT** 128, 129	**DESIGN PROJECT** 130	**KERR/NOBLE** 131
GOLLINGS & PIDGEON 132, 133	**CHRISTINE FENT, GILMAR WENDT** 134	**SAS DESIGN** 134, 135	**PENTAGRAM DESIGN, SAN FRANCISCO** 136	**RB-M** 137	**ATELIER WORKS** 138, 139, 158
Ó! 141	**EXPERIMENTAL JETSET** 142, 159	**LSD** 143, 144, 145	**FIREBELLY DESIGN** 146	**RUSSELL WARREN-FISHER** 147	**SEA** 150
STUDIO MYERSCOUGH 151	**WHY NOT ASSOCIATES** 152	**PENTAGRAM DESIGN, BERLIN** 153	**BOCCALATTE** 154	**VOICE** 155	**PENTAGRAM DESIGN, LONDON** 157

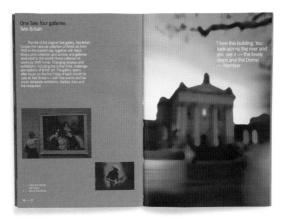

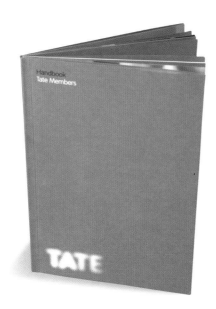

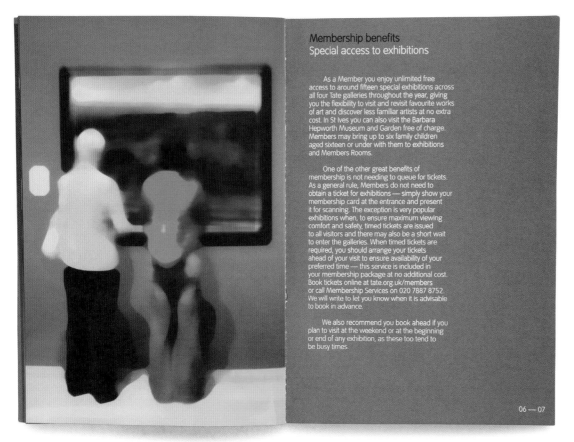

Membership benefits
Special access to exhibitions

As a Member you enjoy unlimited free access to around fifteen special exhibitions across all four Tate galleries throughout the year, giving you the flexibility to visit and revisit favourite works of art and discover less familiar artists at no extra cost. In St Ives you can also visit the Barbara Hepworth Museum and Garden free of charge. Members may bring up to six family children aged sixteen or under with them to exhibitions and Members Rooms.

One of the other great benefits of membership is not needing to queue for tickets. As a general rule, Members do not need to obtain a ticket for exhibitions — simply show your membership card at the entrance and present it for scanning. The exception is very popular exhibitions when, to ensure maximum viewing comfort and safety, timed tickets are issued to all visitors and there may also be a short wait to enter the galleries. When timed tickets are required, you should arrange your tickets ahead of your visit to ensure availability of your preferred time — this service is included in your membership package at no additional cost. Book tickets online at tate.org.uk/members or call Membership Services on 020 7887 8752. We will write to let you know when it is advisable to book in advance.

We also recommend you book ahead if you plan to visit at the weekend or at the beginning or end of any exhibition, as these too tend to be busy times.

06 — 07

NB:STUDIO
**Tate Members
Handbook**

114

Art Directors:
Nick Finney, Ben Stott,
Alan Dye
Designer:
Sarah Fullerton
Client:
Tate

CHENG DESIGN
**Poetry Series
Brochure**

115

Designer:
Karen Cheng
Client:
Seattle Arts
& Lectures
Software:
Adobe InDesign,
Adobe Illustrator
Paper/Materials:
Domtar Titanium

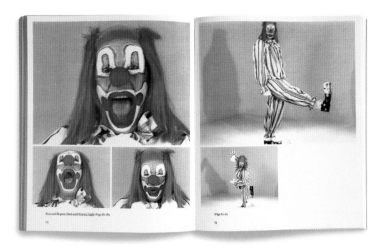

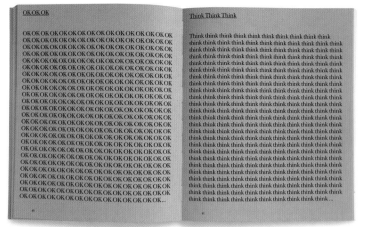

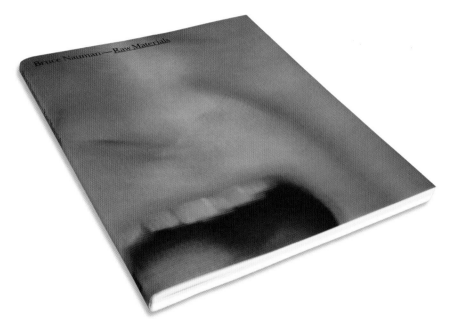

CARTLIDGE
LEVENE
**Bruce Nauman—
Raw Materials**

116

Art Director:
Ian Cartlidge
Designer:
Hector Pottie
Client:
Tate Publishing
Software:
Adobe InDesign

ROSE
The Flower Cabinet Exhibition Catalog
117

Art Director:
Simon Elliott
Designer:
Terry Stephens
Client:
Barbara and
Zafer Baran
Software:
QuarkXPress,
Adobe Photoshop
Paper/Materials:
Consort Royal Satin
250 gsm, Fenner
Redeem 70 gsm

Introduction
BRENT ELLIOTT
Librarian, Royal Horticultural Society

In 2003, the Royal Mail commissioned various artists to produce designs for a set of stamps to commemorate the bicentenary the following year of the Royal Horticultural Society.

After much discussion and various experiments using portraits, garden views, and other ideas, it was decided to make the stamps represent the work of the RHS as an International Cultivar Registration Authority. The international programme of plant name registration was set up in the 1950s, though the RHS had begun registering daffodil names in the first decade of the 20th century, and had begun compiling lists for other sorts of plants in the interim. The scheme works as follows: a breeder, having raised a new variety of a plant, applies to the relevant organisation to have its name registered; the Registration Authority first checks to ensure that the proposed name is not already in use for some other variety of the same plant. For the grower, registration acts as a form of trade... for the gardener, it helps to ensure that... not trade under multiple names... the Society's major inter...

Authority for nine categories of plants, more than any other single organisation: clematis, conifers, daffodils, dahlias, delphiniums, dianthus, lilies, rhododendrons, and orchids.

The six plants chosen for the stamps are a clematis ('Arabella'), a carnation (*Dianthus* Allwoodii Group), a dahlia ('Garden Princess'), a delphinium ('Clifford Sky'), a lily ('Lemon Pixie'), and an orchid (*Miltonia* 'French Lake').

The Society has long been involved in the commissioning and collection of botanical art, from the early days w... published hand-coloured engravings in it... to the present day when it holds bo... at its winter flower shows. T... been awarded its Ve... century, an... the...

Barbara and Zafer Baran
The Flower Cabinet

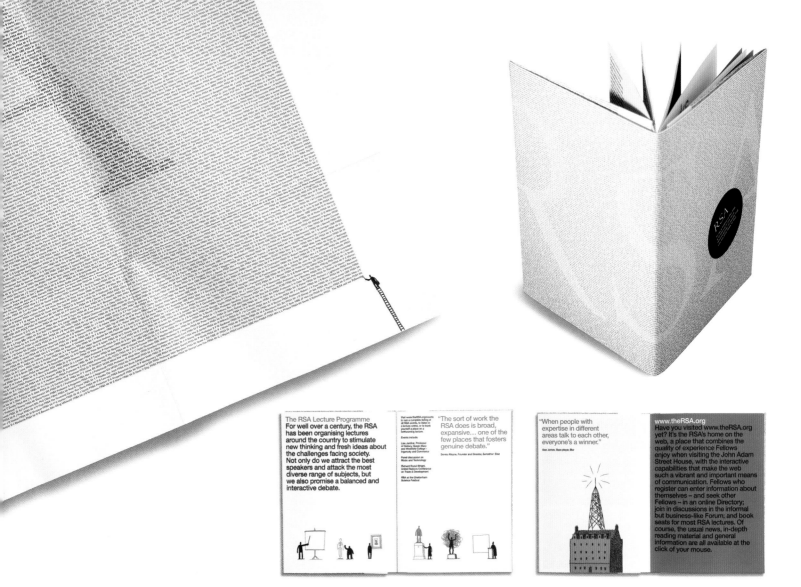

RSA Projects

The RSA delivers its mission through a portfolio of interdisciplinary projects, whose current aim is the advancement of a society keen on creativity and its principled exploitation. In particular the Programme aims to encourage innovation and invention; to help both the technology and the arts-based industries, to improve the national competence (knowledge, skills and behaviours); and to improve and extend professional standards.

The Society supports this activity by obtaining sponsorship from a diverse range of sources. Important among these is the expertise, effort and financial contribution of its Fellows. For more information, visit www.theRSA.org/projects

Project 1
Can the professions survive? – professional values for the 21st century
There is a widespread perception that the professions are under threat. No longer able to claim special privileges as disinterested, altruistic occupational groups acting detachedly in the public interest, professions are finding their traditional values and loyalties eroded.

In this climate, can – and should – the professions survive?

We are establishing a new project that seeks to consider some of these issues. The overall aim of the project is to re-invigorate the concept of a 'profession', to enlarge its application and to encourage the professions in the UK to become a more significant, trusted, and creative force for economic and social good.

The Comino Foundation has contributed towards the costs of this project.

Project 2
Science, Citizenship and the Market
This project is a major element of the RSA's move to strengthen its interventions in manufactures and commerce. All industry depends on a continuing flow of new science to maintain its product and process base but, as the recent GM controversy made clear, science-based industries ignore public opinion and perception at their peril. The failure to anticipate public reactions to a new technology can be expensive and damaging both for companies and for society.

We have made a significant investment to establish a project that will investigate the ways in which companies can benefit from incorporating socially sensitive antennae into their decision-making framework. One of the strengths of the project will lie in the collaboration between the RSA and a leading university: the project is being developed by the Science and Technology Studies Department of University College, London.

Project 3
The Economy of the Imagination
'The Economy of the Imagination' project, inspired by the New Statesman Lecture given by Lord Evans of the same title, aims to "find the line where high culture and commerce can meet to mutual advantage," as he put it. By examining each arts-based industry in turn, we will identify risk-takers who shun the easy temptation to produce formulaic, market-oriented products and support more innovative works. It is this risk-taking that we want to encourage.

www.theRSA.org/projects

NB:STUDIO
RSA New Members Handbook

118

Art Directors:
Nick Finney, Ben Stott, Alan Dye
Designers:
Nick Vincent, Tom Gauld
Client:
RSA

BLUE RIVER
**Programme
Launch**

119

Designers:
James Askham,
Neil Southern,
Anthony Cantwell
Client:
BALTIC Centre for
Contemporary Art
Software:
Adobe Photoshop,
QuarkXPress
Paper|Materials:
THINK 4 Bright

TOMATO KOŠIR S.P.
Jazz Festival
Ljubljana

120

Art Director:
Tomato Košir
Designer:
Tomato Košir
Client:
Cankarjev Dom
Software:
Adobe Photoshop,
Adobe Illustrator
Paper/Materials:
Hello Matt

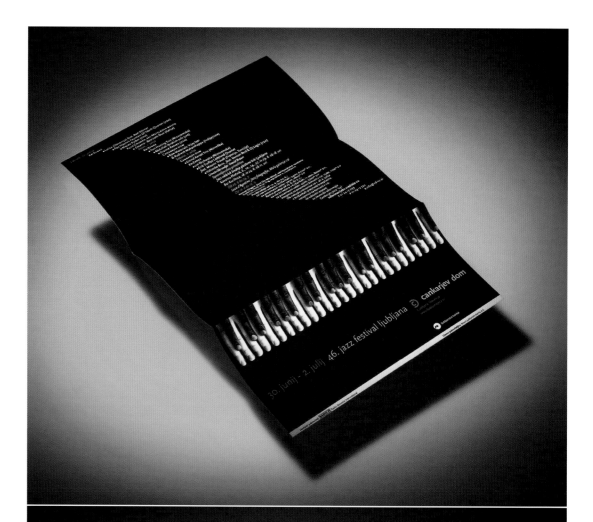

Guillermo Santamarina: Tras una pausa de más de 50 a[ños]
recupera el invento de Daniel Mont al que su tal[ento]
dio forma, activó prematuramente, y den[...]
de Mont, la visión y la astucia de [...]
La continuidad de la m[...]
Gabriel Orozco [...]
creación conte[...]
caracterizó la t[...]
sin duda dos d[...]

[...] entender los conflictos del proyecto de *El Eco* y en
[...] como la de otros artistas de esa época.
[...] sería más productivo analizar
[...] [...]nales

Gabriel Orozco, "Ba[...]

Gabriel Orozc[o]
que sería buen[...]
Carlos Amoral[es...]
al estado filos[...]
hace referenci[...]
está construid[...]
Facultad de A[...]
con la vocació[n...]

GO: Desde luego. En mi caso, y creo que también en el de Damián y de Carlos, la relación con Mathias Goeritz no es tan estrecha. La reapertura de este espacio no me fue planteada como un homenaje, y la invitación que se nos hace es con la intención de revitalizarlo para su contemporaneidad, para darle un impulso hacia un futuro posible y que no se convierta en un espacio nostálgico. El hecho de que se me invitara a realizar este proyecto conociendo la distancia y la brecha generacional, ya provoca de entrada algo interesante. Se reabre un espacio mítico a una discusión contemporánea, y esto en su nuevo y relevante contexto universitario, el cual me parece perfecto.

Damián Ortega, "Crítica al estado filosófico: Papalotes Negros", 2004 (Foto de la obra en proceso).

GS: La misión y la programación de este museo experimental consideran la perspectiva substancial de aquel *El Eco* que puede reconocerse como contenedor de movimiento humano cumplidamente razonable y conveniente, contrario a la coerción nacionalista que pretendía arraigarse infinitamente dentro de la cultura de México. Su breve historia, acompañada de críticas feroces y de envidia, indica que hubo afortunadamente un grupo de personas sensatas que veían más allá de esa condición aislada, y con sanas intenciones de legitimar una red de comunicación mundial. Con la muerte de Daniel Mont, la tragedia ensombreció su destino, y a eso debe sumarse que sus

BURGEFF DESIGN
ELECO
Experimental
Museum
121

Art Director:
Patrick Burgeff
Designer:
Patrick Burgeff
Client:
Direccion General de
Artes Visuales UNAM
Software:
FreeHand,
Adobe Photoshop
Paper/Materials:
Couche 300 gr

Robbie Sparks

LIPPA PEARCE
**Circular 12,
Issue 12**

122

Art Director:
Domenic Lippa
Designer:
Domenic Lippa
Client:
The Typographic
Circle

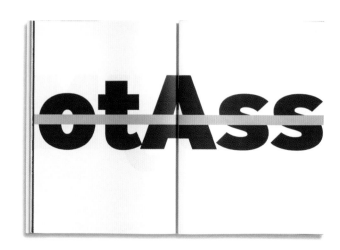

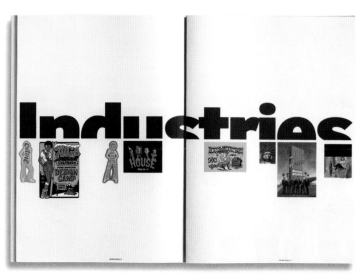

SAGMEISTER INC.
**The Guggenheim,
Douglas Gordon**

123

Art Director:
Stefan Sagmeister
Designer:
Matthias Ernstberger
Typography:
Marian Bantjes
Production:
Lara Fieldbinder,
Melissa Secundino
Writer:
Nancy Spector
Client:
The Guggenheim
Museum, Berlin
Software:
Adobe CS
Paper/Materials:
Postcards

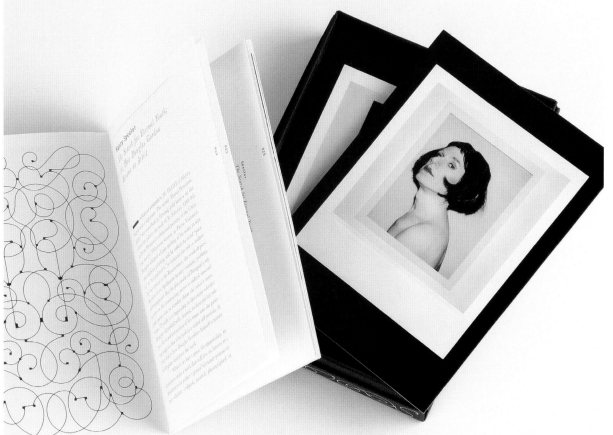

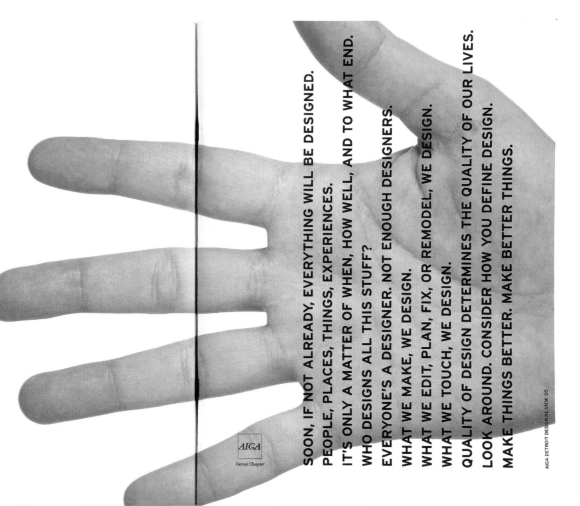

SOON, IF NOT ALREADY, EVERYTHING WILL BE DESIGNED.
PEOPLE, PLACES, THINGS, EXPERIENCES.
IT'S ONLY A MATTER OF WHEN, HOW WELL, AND TO WHAT END.
WHO DESIGNS ALL THIS STUFF?
EVERYONE'S A DESIGNER. NOT ENOUGH DESIGNERS.
WHAT WE MAKE, WE DESIGN.
WHAT WE EDIT, PLAN, FIX, OR REMODEL, WE DESIGN.
WHAT WE TOUCH, WE DESIGN.
QUALITY OF DESIGN DETERMINES THE QUALITY OF OUR LIVES.
LOOK AROUND. CONSIDER HOW YOU DEFINE DESIGN.
MAKE THINGS BETTER. MAKE BETTER THINGS.

AIGA DETROIT DESIGN RE:VIEW .05

AIGA

AIGA
Detroit Chapter

BEST

BBK STUDIO
**AIGA Detroit
Design Re:View
'05 Awards Book**

124

Art Director:
Kevin Budelmann
Designers:
Brian Hauch,
Jason Murray
Client:
AIGA Detroit
Software:
Adobe Illustrator,
Adobe Photoshop,
QuarkXPress

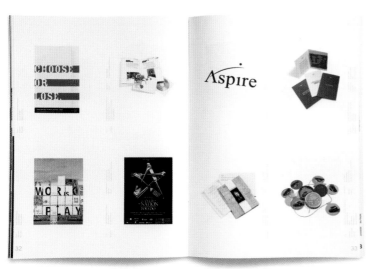

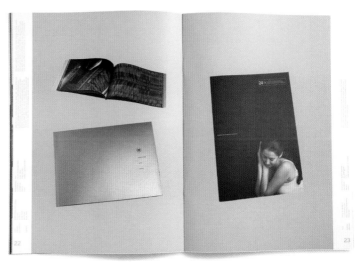

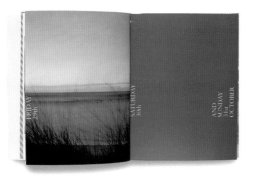

BILLY BLUE CREATIVE,
PRECINCT
AGDA Awards
Invite to Sydney

125

Art Directors:
Justin Smith,
Geordie McKenzie
Designers:
Justin Smith,
Geordie McKenzie
Client:
AGDA
Software:
Adobe Illustrator,
Adobe Photoshop,
QuarkXPress

BC, MH
JAMES LAMBERT
Monika Sosnowska
Art Pack

126

Designers:
Ben Chatfield,
Mark Hopkins,
James Lambert
Client:
Serpentine Gallery
Software:
Adobe Illustrator,
QuarkXPress
Paper/Materials:
Beer Mat Board

VIVA DOLAN
COMMUNICATIONS
& DESIGN INC.
Prospectus Brochure
127

Art Director:
Frank Viva
Designer:
Todd Temporate
Client:
The Interior
Design Show
Software:
QuarkXPress
Paper/Materials:
Knightkote Matte
80 lb text cover

Exterior Design

THIS SPECIAL SECTION SHOWCASES LANDSCAPE ARCHITECTS, DESIGNERS,
DESIGNER-BUILDERS, AND MANUFACTURERS AND DISTRIBUTORS OF OUTDOOR
LIVING, FURNITURE, ORNAMENTAL METAL AND ARCHITECTURAL PRODUCTS

2005
The Interior Design Show
LIVING DESIGN

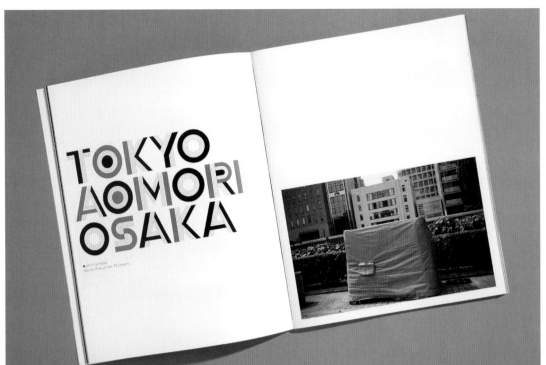

Art Director:
Sander Vermeulen
Designers:
Sander Vermeulen,
Annelies Vaneyden,
Ian Boric
Client:
Hiawatha
Paper|Materials:
Bioton, Artic Volume,
Munken Lynx, Artic
Silk, Amber Graphic

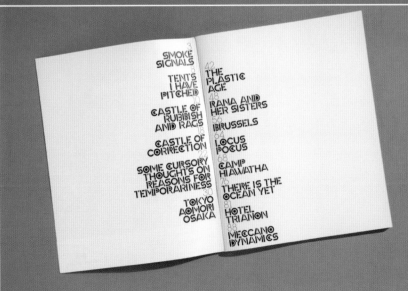

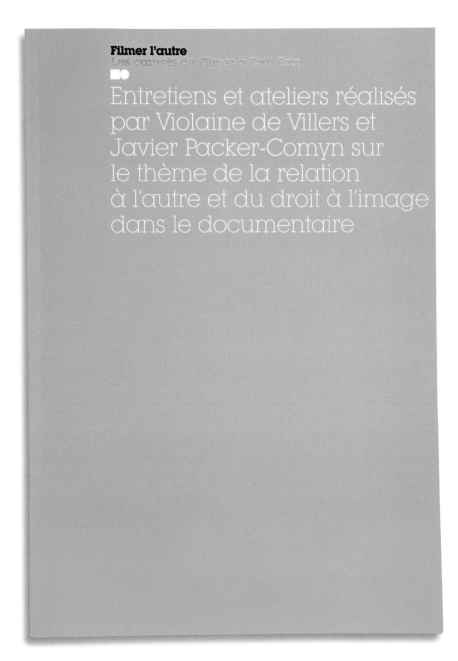

Filmer l'autre
Les carnets de Filmer à Tout Prix

Entretiens et ateliers réalisés
par Violaine de Villers et
Javier Packer-Comyn sur
le thème de la relation
à l'autre et du droit à l'image
dans le documentaire

FANCLUBPROJECT
Notes of a
Discussion Group

129

Art Director:
Sander Vermeulen
Designer:
Sander Vermeulen
Client:
Filmer l'autre
Paper/Materials:
Offset

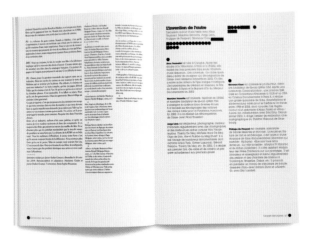

DESIGN PROJECT
**Situation Leeds
Festival Guide**

130

Art Directors:
Andy Probert,
James Littlewood
Designers:
Andy Probert,
James Littlewood
Client:
Situation Leeds
Software:
QuarkXPress,
Freehand
Paper/Materials:
Kaskad Flamingo
Pink, Raflatac
Glossprint (Robert
Horne)

Artist(s)/title: **Nichola Pemberton**

Over Hearing

Number/category: **#29/Festival project**

Description: **Based on customer conversations this scripted performance piece is read by four actors. Not presented obviously, it mimics regular customers leaving the viewer to experience the café and wonder which overheard conversations are contrived.**

Date/time/location:

**Mon 23 May to
Fri 27 May
2:30—3:30pm**

**Four Cousins Grille
and Coffee Lounge
10 Market St
Arcade
Leeds LS1 6DH**

Artist(s)/title: **Roland Piché**

The World Trade Center Memorial Competition: A Proposal by Roland Piché

Number/category: **#30/Festival project**

Description: **Drawings, maquettes and a film detailing Roland Piché's proposal for a memorial to victims of the 9/11 atrocity. The competition attracted more than five thousand entrants from all over the world, including fifty one from Britain. This exhibition highlights the processes and pitfalls of involvement in such a high-profile event.**

Date/time/location:

**Thurs 12 May to
Tues 31 May
Mon to Sun
10am—5:30pm
Wed 10am—9pm**

**Henry Moore
Institute
74 The Headrow
Leeds LS1 3AH**

**Disabled access
available**

**0113 246 9469
matthew@henry-moore.ac.uk**

Situation Leeds locator map for exhibitions and events.
Plan your route around the festival and use the stickers below to highlight the projects or talks that you want to see. Just peel off a sticker and stick it in the circle shown on each page.
It's an easy way to make sure that you don't miss out on the many enjoyable and interesting experiences at the festival.

Festival locator map

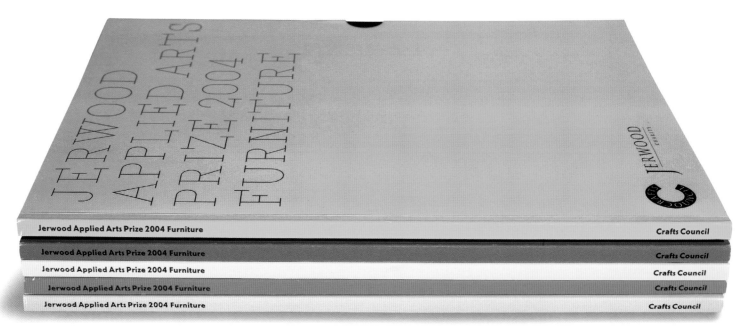

KERR/NOBLE
**Jerwood Furniture
Prize Catalog**

131

Art Director:
Kerr/Noble
Designer:
Kerr/Noble
Client:
Crafts Council

GOLLINGS
& PIDGEON
**The Plot
Thickens Catalog**
132

Art Director:
David Pidgeon
Designer:
Marianna Berek-Lewis
Client:
Heide Museum of
Modern Art
Software:
QuarkXPress
Paper/Materials:
Freelife Vellum White,
Encore Super Gloss
Recycled

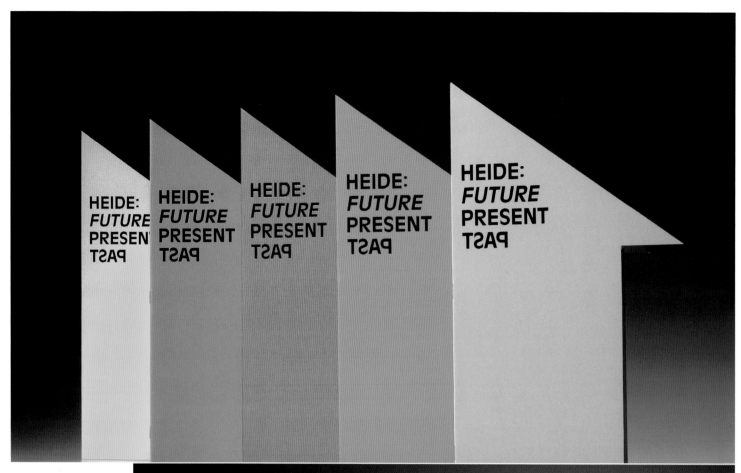

GOLLINGS
& PIDGEON
**Future Present
Past Catalog**

133

Art Director:
David Pidgeon
Designer:
Tina Chen
Client:
Heide Museum of
Modern Art
Software:
Adobe InDesign
Paper/Materials:
Optix: Inga Turquoise,
Suni Yellow, Janz
Orange, Reva Green,
Raza Red, Monza
Satin Recycled

Art Directors:
Christine Fent,
Hanja Hellpap,
Gilmar Wendt
Designers:
Christine Fent,
Hanja Hellpap,
Gilmar Wendt
Client:
STD
Software:
QuarkXPress
Paper/Materials:
Hanno Art Matt

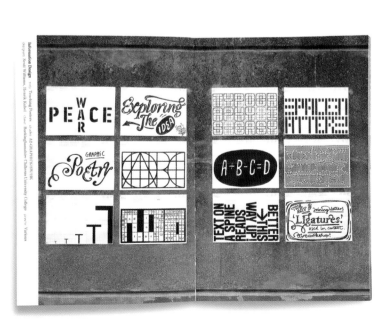

SAS DESIGN
BT Connected
Worlds Arts
Project Madrid
135

Art Director:
Gilmar Wendt
Designer:
Rosanna Vitiello
Client:
BT
Software:
QuarkXPress
Paper/Materials:
Colorplan Plain
Finish Pristine White
(cover), Munken
Print Extra Vol 18
Parilux Gloss (text)

¿Para qué necesitamos el arte en las ciudades? Un recorrido histórico permite decir que las artes, y en general los recursos estéticos, son necesarios no sólo por razones ornamentales sino en otros sentidos más decisivos. Encuentro al menos cuatro fines con los cuales el arte, la literatura y los medios masivos han intervenido e intervienen en espacios urbanos: para fundarlos y refundarlos, para celebrar, para espectacularizar y para nombrar u ocultar su pérdida. Néstor García Canclini

Why do we need art in cities? If we look at history we can see that the arts, and aesthetic resources in general, are necessary not just for ornamental purposes but also for more important reasons. I can identify at least four motivating factors which underlie the continuing intervention of art, literature and the mass media in urban spaces: to create and recreate these spaces, to celebrate them, to make them more spectacular, and to pinpoint or conceal their loss. Néstor García Canclini

PENTAGRAM DESIGN,
SAN FRANCISCO
AIGA Design Legends Gala Program
136

Art Director:
Kit Hinrichs
Designer:
Jessica Siegel
Client:
AIGA
Software:
Adobe InDesign
Paper/Materials:
Sappi McCoy, Cougar

The Design Legends Gala is a nascent tradition, in only its second year, and already a celebratory occasion for all who respect the importance of the great design legacy. The gala is an opportunity for the community of designers to gather and honor those who have come before and whose creativity, inspiration, innovation and brilliant execution have defined the profession and every young designer's ambitions. This is an event where old friendships are renewed, new friendships are created and everyone is in awe of the sheer talent of the design profession.

FOR OVER 80 YEARS, THE AIGA MEDAL HAS BEEN AWARDED TO THE FEW WHO SET THE STANDARDS OF EXCELLENCE FOR DESIGN.

RB-M
**Suky Best/
Artist's Publication**

137

Designer:
Richard
Bonner-Morgan
Client:
Film & Video Umbrella
Software:
QuarkXPress
Paper/Materials:
Neptune Unique,
Fenner Paper

Art Director:
Quentin Newark
Designer:
S. Bechtolf
Client:
Tate Britain
Software:
Adobe Photoshop,
QuarkXPress

Exposed
The Victorian Nude

TATE

Robert Davies

Epiphany

It is often in the detail of life that significance occurs. Detail is everything. From the way the rivets on a Spitfire were flattened to enhance its speed to the corners of the mouth on Leonardo's Mona Lisa. The weight of Pele's pass to Carlos Alberto...

Robert Davies

Epiphany

Each image describes a moment of instinctive grace or wit, triumph or tragedy, which transported an audience. Both figurative and abstract, these are glimpses of ephemeral things. Yet each is a moment of revelation, an epiphany.

Beckham
England v Argentina
2 - 2 (Last 16)
30th June 1998
Att. 36,000
Stade Geoffroy Guichard, St. Etienne, France

Owen
England v Argentina
2 - 2 (Last 16)
30th June 1998
Att. 36,000
Stade Geoffroy Guichard, St. Etienne, France

Tilkowski
England v West Germany
4 - 2 (Final)
30th July 1966
Att. 96,924
Wembley, London, England

Charlton / Tilkowski
England v West Germany
4 - 2 (Final)
30th July 1966
Att. 96,924
Wembley, London, England

Art Director:
Ian Chilvers
Designer:
Ian Chilvers
Client:
The Blue Gallery
Software:
QuarkXPress

{ 2005-2006
Seattle Arts & Lectures
SPECIAL EVENTS }

AN EVENING WITH CHARLES JENCKS

WILDERNESS AND IMAGINATION:
SUBHANKAR BANERJEE, TERRY TEMPEST WILLIAMS,
AND DAVID ALLEN SIBLEY

Presented by Seattle Arts & Lectures and the Seattle Art Museum
Underwritten by NBBJ and Sellen Construction Company
with support from Reed, Longyear, Malnati, Ahrens & West, PLLC

Presented by Seattle Arts & Lectures and North Cascades Institute
Underwritten by the Consulate General of Canada and the Lannan Foundation
with assistance from The Mountaineers Books

WEDNESDAY NOVEMBER 2, 7:30PM
ILLSLEY BALL NORDSTROM RECITAL HALL, BENAROYA HALL
GENERAL ADMISSION-$15
SEATTLE ART MUSEUM MEMBERS-$12 • STUDENTS/UNDER 25-$7.50

TUESDAY DECEMBER 6, 7:30PM
S. MARK TAPER FOUNDATION AUDITORIUM, BENAROYA HALL
PATRON SEATING-$50 • MAIN FLOOR-$25
BALCONY-$20 • STUDENTS/UNDER 25-$10

Renowned architect and theorist Charles Jencks is most famous for his writings on postmodern architecture. His influential book *The Language of Post-Modern Architecture* (1977) extended the concept of postmodernism from literary criticism to the visual arts. He is author of more than thirty books, including *Towards a Symbolic Architecture* (1985), *The Architecture of the Jumping Universe* (1995), and *The Garden of Cosmic Speculation* (2003). His most recent book, *The Iconic Building*, analyzes world-famous structures by Frank Gehry, Daniel Libeskind, and Rem Koolhaas, among other leading architects. Jencks's own innovative work includes the dramatic and radical landscaping project, Landform, for the Scottish National Gallery of Modern Art.

Charles Jencks divides his time among lecturing, writing, and designing in the United States, the United Kingdom, Europe, and Asia. He earned degrees in English literature and architecture at Harvard and in architectural history at the University of London. He lives in Scotland.

Please join us for a special evening featuring internationally acclaimed Arctic photographer Subhankar Banerjee; noted ornithologist, bird illustrator, and author David Allen Sibley; and poet and environmental activist Terry Tempest Williams. "Wilderness and Imagination" focuses on the vital relationship of natural resources and culture. The three speakers offer richly nuanced views of nature. Terry Tempest Williams's book *Refuge: An Unnatural History of Family and Place* (1991) is cited as a classic of American nature writing. Preservationists consider *The Sibley Guide to Birds* (2000) a monumental achievement. Subhankar Banerjee took the breathtaking photos featured in the exhibit *Arctic National Wildlife Refuge: Seasons of Life and Land*, on display at the Burke Museum of Natural History and Culture in Seattle. The speakers will reflect on philosophical, literary, and visual presentations of nature. They will comment on ways in which the natural world has historically been perceived and consumed in our society, as well as the resulting impact on environmental policies.

"Charles Jencks is unequivocally architecture's greatest living storyteller."—Architecture

"We call out—and the land calls back."—Terry Tempest Williams

CHENG DESIGN
**Literary Lectures
Series 2005–2006**

140

Designer:
Karen Cheng
Client:
Seattle Arts
& Lectures
Software:
Adobe InDesign,
Adobe Illustrator
Paper/Materials:
Domtar Titanium

{ 2005-2006
Seattle Arts & Lectures
LITERARY LECTURE SERIES }

CYNTHIA OZICK
SIMON WINCHESTER
ALEXANDER McCALL SMITH
PAUL AUSTER
AZAR NAFISI
PETER MATTHIESSEN

ALEXANDER McCALL SMITH

7:30PM BENAROYA HALL • MONDAY NOVEMBER 14
UNDERWRITTEN BY CHRISTENSEN O'CONNOR JOHNSON KINDNESS PLLC

PAUL AUSTER

7:30PM BENAROYA HALL • MONDAY JANUARY 23
UNDERWRITTEN BY GULL INDUSTRIES

"Sweet, soothing novels...valued for their healing properties."
—The New York Times

"Prose unfailingly limpid, supple, and energetic."
—The Wall Street Journal

As the creator of the utterly charming series *The No. 1 Ladies' Detective Agency*, the Scottish lawyer and author Alexander McCall Smith enjoys a loyal worldwide following. McCall Smith was born in Zimbabwe and taught law in Botswana, the rich backdrop for the Ladies' Detective series. Generous in wit and spirit, Precious Ramotswe solves cases not of violent crime but of domestic messiness—an overstrict father, wayward teenager, and cheating husband. Our sensible lady detective concludes, "All men carried on with the ladies, in her experience."

The versatile and erudite McCall Smith has published more than fifty books, from academic texts such as *Law and Medical Ethics* (2003) to African folktales and children's stories such as *Akimbo and the Elephant* (2005). A second light-footed series, *Portuguese Irregular Verbs* (2003), features the punctilious Professor Dr. Moritz-Maria von Igfelfeld, who "often reflected on how fortunate he was to be exactly who he was, and nobody else." The latest series of witty mysteries, *The Sunday Philosophy Club*, traces the cozy life of the high-minded heroine Isabel Dalhousie in titles as irresistible as *Friends, Lovers, and Chocolate* (2005), that fans hope he will overtake the one-hundred-book record of P.G. Wodehouse, his predecessor in sparkling farce.

McCall Smith teaches medical law at the University of Edinburgh. An amateur bassoonist, he co-founded and performs with "The Really Terrible Orchestra" in his spare time.

The prolific novelist, essayist, poet, and screenwriter Paul Auster mines the themes of shifting identity, arbitrary influence, and elusive truth. Auster sees life as filled with "unexpected events and strange twists," a view reinforced by a pivotal event in his own life, when as a fourteen-year-old he went hiking with a friend who was killed by lightning. Swayed by mysterious coincidences, Auster's characters navigate surreal settings as they search for meaning and identity. In *The Book of Illusions* (2002), the discovery of a blue notebook containing a mystery affects a man's grief over the sudden death of his family. Other critical favorites among his ten novels are *The New York Trilogy* (1985-86), *Oracle Night* (2004), and *The Music of Chance* (1990), nominated for the PEN/Faulkner Award. In the 1990s, Auster branched into screenwriting for *Smoke*, *Blue in the Face*, and *Lulu on the Bridge*, which he also directed. Memoirs and essays round out his considerable body of work.

After earning an M.A. from Columbia, Auster assumed the role of starving artist, scraping out a living as a census taker, translator, and merchant seaman. Described by one critic as a "Francophile existentialist with a touch of Gothic," he enjoys a strong following in France, where he lived in his twenties. Auster has received the French Prix Medicis for Foreign Literature as well as a National Endowment for the Arts fellowship.

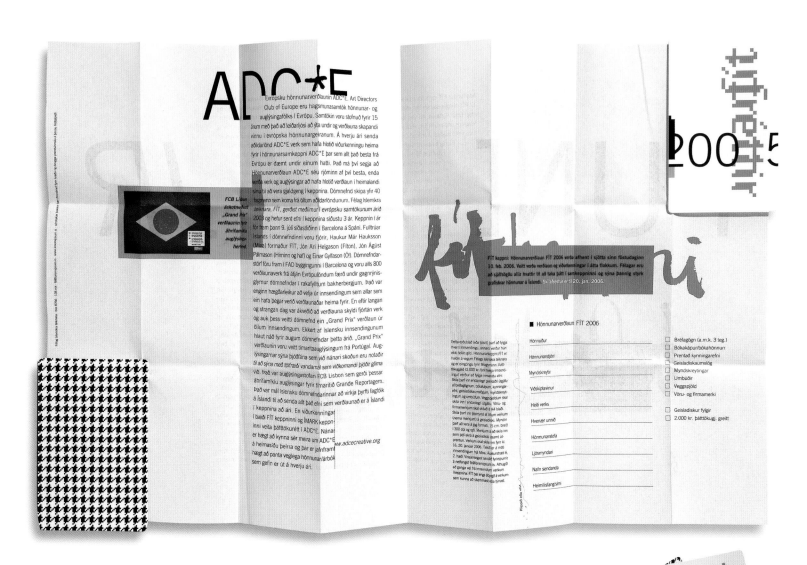

Ó!

Newsletter for FIT

141

Art Director:
Einar Gylfason
Designer:
Einar Gylfason
Client:
FIT, Association of
Icelandic Graphic
Designers
Software:
Freehand
Paper/Materials:
California duo 400 gr,
Z-opaque W type R
50 gr

EXPERIMENTAL
JETSET
Time and Again

142

Art Director:
Experimental Jetset
Designer:
Experimental Jetset
Client:
Stedelijk Museum

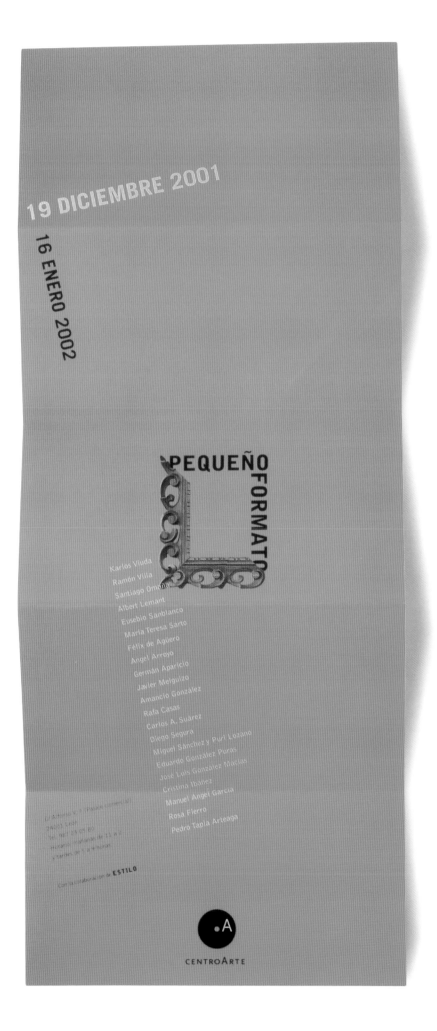

LSD
Promotional Pamphlets for an Art Gallery
143

Art Directors:
Sonia Díaz,
Gabriel Martínez
Designers:
Sonia Díaz,
Gabriel Martínez
Client:
Centroarte
Software:
Adobe Photoshop,
Freehand
Paper/Materials:
Offset on different
papers

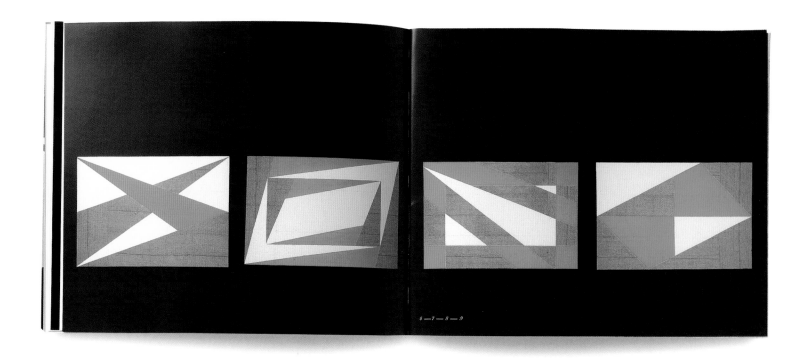

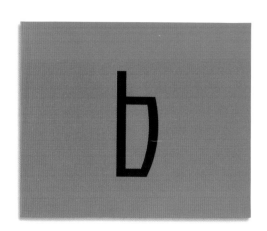

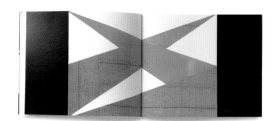

¿Cómo puede ocurrir que lo que subyuga nuestra imaginación, disguste a nuestros ojos? DIDEROT

La primera vez que abordé la obra de EB ·ahora hace un año· realicé algunas consideraciones sobre el ascetismo de su mirada, que limitaba los materiales y reducía los elementos puestos en juego en su trabajo pictórico.

Me llamó la atención su texto explicativo "Apuntes sobre pespuntes", en el que mostraba la capacidad de reflexionar sobre su propia obra y en el que aludía a un cierto grado cero barthesiano de su trabajo, como un proceso abierto y en revisión. Frente a la tentación creciente del exceso expresivo y de la acumulación de significados, me llamó poderosamente la atención ese ejercicio de contención que emparenta con la sentencia de Mies van der Rohe "Less is more". Navegar hoy, además, en aguas de la abstracción geométrica en tiempos presididos por otros rumbos neofigurativos o por otros rumbos sin norte alguno, era, tal vez, un síntoma de osadía marinera o un propósito descabellado, que no restaban rigor y misterio a un proceso en formación y a un trabajo enraizado en las experiencias de los Neoplasticistas holandeses y en los Suprematistas soviéticos de la segunda década del siglo.

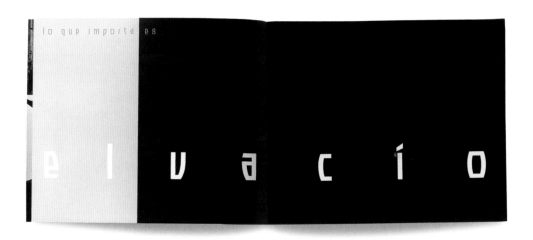

LSD
Artist's
Promotional
Brochure
144

Art Directors:
Sonia Díaz,
Gabriel Martínez
Designers:
Sonia Díaz,
Gabriel Martínez
Client:
Eduardo Barco
Software:
Adobe Photoshop,
Freehand
Paper/Materials:
Offset

Art Director:
Gabriel Martínez
Designer:
Gabriel Martínez
Client:
El Milano Real
Software:
Freehand
Paper/Materials:
Offset

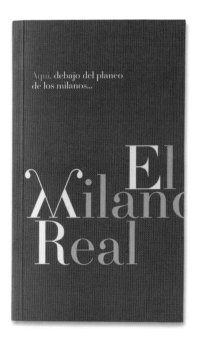

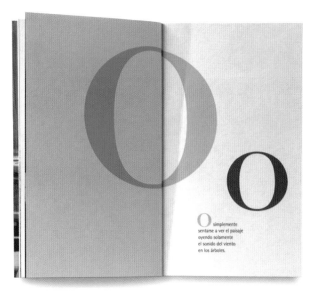

Anchor Graphics

Anchor Graphics works in the areas of visual arts and arts education for youth, adult, and professional artists. We are a community-based nonprofit printshop and gallery that brings together, under professional guidance, a diverse community of youth, emerging and established artists, and the public to advance the fine art of printmaking by integrating education with the creation of prints. For over fourteen years, Anchor Graphics has offered educational programs, exhibitions, and artist services revolving around the history and practice of printmaking. Anchor Graphics is a printshop, which functions as both a classroom and an atelier, fulfilling the need for affordable access to a properly equipped shop, while maintaining a focus on education within a professional artistic environment. As a non-profit organization, our ethos is three-fold. First, Anchor Graphics maintains an environment in which artists of all experience and age levels are welcome, encouraged to explore and be innovative with the printmaking medium, and supported in realizing their own creative visions. We offer open studio time that allows artists of various skill levels to work under the guidance of master printers, and an Artist-in-Residency program that brings experienced artist/printmakers from across the country to Chicago to share

their knowledge and work. Second, Anchor Graphics mentors Chicagoland area youth. By introducing them to printmaking and educating them in the discipline through Press-On-Wheels workshops and high school classes, we are equipping them with fundamental life tools. Through the creation of original images and the running of professional hand presses we are teaching young people the value of cooperation and sequential planning. All of our high school classes and workshops are free to the students. We also hire interns from various colleges every year and train them in all aspects of running a nonprofit printshop and gallery. Finally, we are committed to educating the community at large about printmaking. Through exhibitions, lectures, demonstrations, and adult classes we are making this art form accessible to anyone who wishes to learn about printmaking's process and history.

04 + 05 / 48

FIREBELLY DESIGN
Artist/Nonprofit Brochure

146

Art Director:
Dawn Hancock
Designers:
Dawn Hancock,
Brent Maynard
Client:
Anchor Graphics/JET
Software:
Adobe Photoshop,
Adobe Illustrator,
Adobe InDesign
Paper/Materials:
Sappi McCoy Velvet

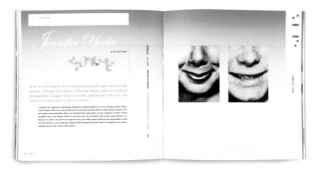

RUSSELL
WARREN-FISHER
**21 Years of
Complicite**
147

Designer:
Russell Warren-Fisher
Client:
Complicite
Software:
QuarkXPress,
Adobe Photoshop

Art Directors:
Nick Finney, Ben Stott,
Alan Dye
Designer:
Jodie Whiteman
Client:
The Hub

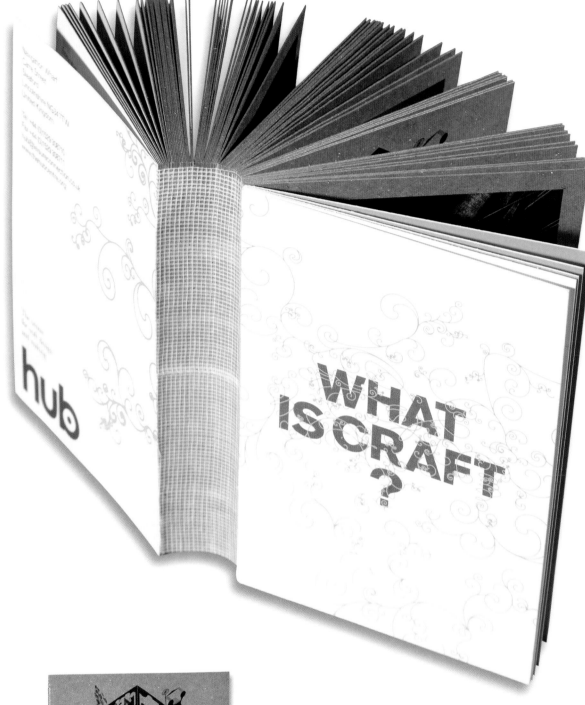

Maker:
Mary Butcher
Nature/Photographer:
Geraldine Rudge,
Editor, Crafts

Willow Line

2003
Materials:
Willow

26

Your choice?
Mary Butcher's 'Willow Line'
gives traditional materials a
contemporary form. The rhythmic
patterns of basketwork have
been abstracted into something
fresh, eye-catching but at the
same time pleasingly familiar.

What is Craft?
Craft is simply skill. It plays
a role in every visual art from
painting to product design.
There was a time when craft
was seen only as handwork
and restricted to the making
of functional objects. In the
new millennium it is resuming
its older role, flowing happily
over boundaries between fine
and applied arts.

NB:STUDIO
Schweppes
Photographic
Portrait Prize
149

Art Directors:
Nick Finney, Ben Stott,
Alan Dye
Designer:
Ian Pierce
Client:
National Portrait
Gallery

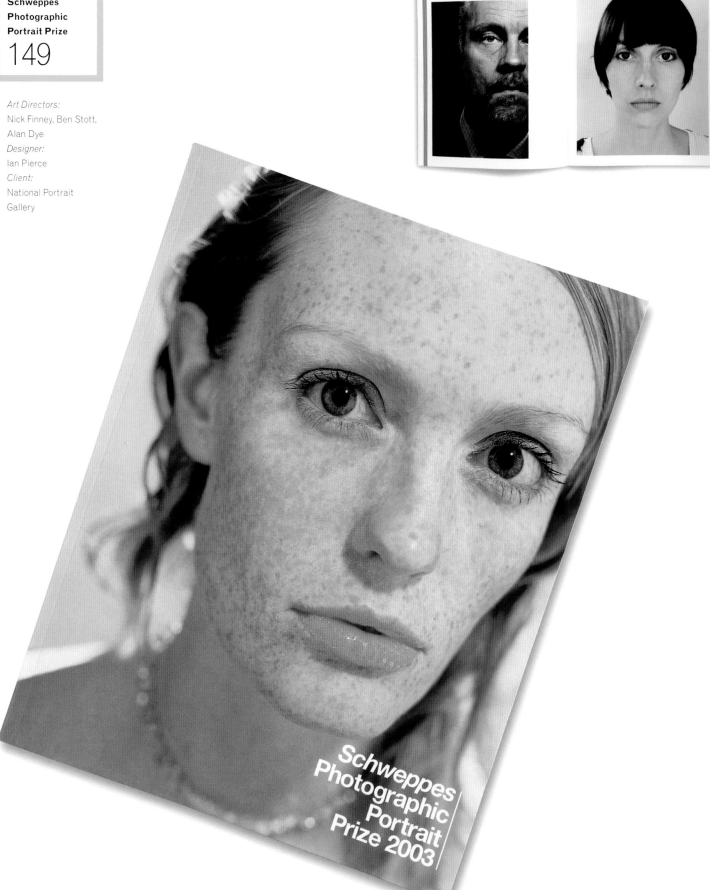

Schweppes
Photographic
Portrait
Prize 2003

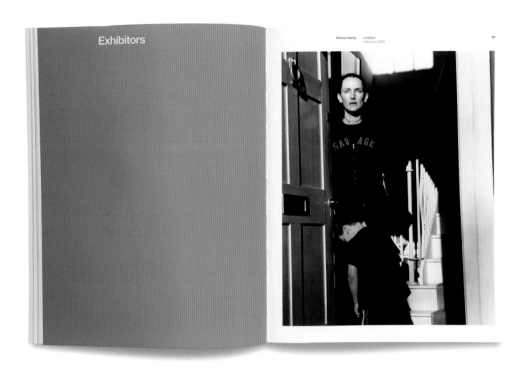

Exhibitors

Emma Hardy   Untitled
February 2003

17

Deloitte Award
Winner
David Yeo

Deloitte.

6   14

David Yeo   Brothers and
Sisters from the
series Family
Members
May 2003

15

Winner of the Deloitte Award for best portrait taken by a photographer aged twenty-five or under, David Yeo graduated this summer with a Diploma in Foundation Photography from Filton College in Bristol. Aged nineteen, he has won the portrait prize with his first ever entry in a photographic competition.

Unlike other students on his course who were creating 'very odd, experimental work' for their graduation shows, Yeo opted for a 'simpler and more straightforward' approach. Wanting to document the various generations of his family, he produced a series of portraits titled Family Members. His winning portrait, Brothers and Sisters, is taken from the series, and shows his three cousins Jeffrey, Sam and Rebecca.

'I come from a very close-knit family and I wanted to capture all of us in a series of photographs before my grandparents died,' he explains. 'Rebecca's brothers are very protective towards her and I think the portrait reflects that. She has an amazing, solemn face, but looks so different from her brothers. I wanted to explore notions of resemblance as well as our close family ties.'

Influenced by Sally Mann's Immediate Family, Yeo set out to create a similar mood of 'dreamy detachment', while at the same time developing his own individual style. Using a wide-angled lens, Yeo took the photograph with a Mamiya and printed on warm-tone paper. 'Technically, my pictures are quite different from Sally Mann's. I shoot outdoors in natural light like she does, but I go in far closer. I prefer much sharper focus, and want as much detail as possible.'

With the photograph's similarities to Calvin Klein and Christian Dior ad campaigns, it's perhaps no surprise that Yeo is considering a career as a fashion photographer. After a trip to Brazil next year, he hopes either to study in New York or to take up a place at the London College of Fashion.

'Fashion has drifted more and more towards portraiture over the past decade, with less and less emphasis on the actual clothes. That's something I would like to reverse,' he says. 'I'd like to have the same kind of impact as Juergen Teller. His approach is very different from mine, all bold flashes and abstraction, but he's turned fashion photography into an art form.'

Interviewed by Richard McClure

Art Director:
Bryan Edmondson
Designer:
Ryan Jones
Client:
Rankin
Software:
QuarkXPress,
Adobe Photoshop
Paper/Materials:
Naturalis

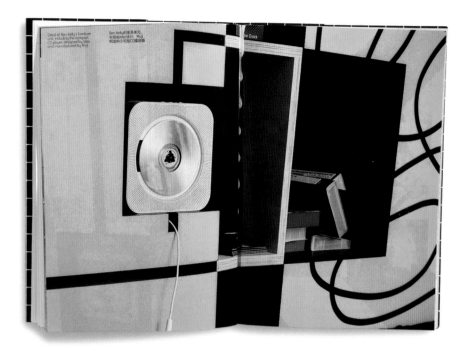

STUDIO
MYERSCOUGH
Hometime

151

Art Director:
Morag Myerscough
Designer:
Morag Myerscough
Photographer:
Richard Learoyd
Client:
British Council

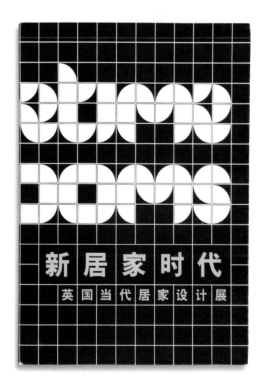

新居家时代
英国当代居家设计展

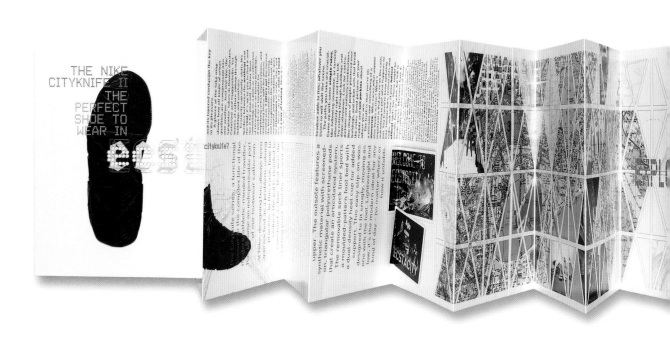

Client:
Nike UK
Software:
Freehand MX

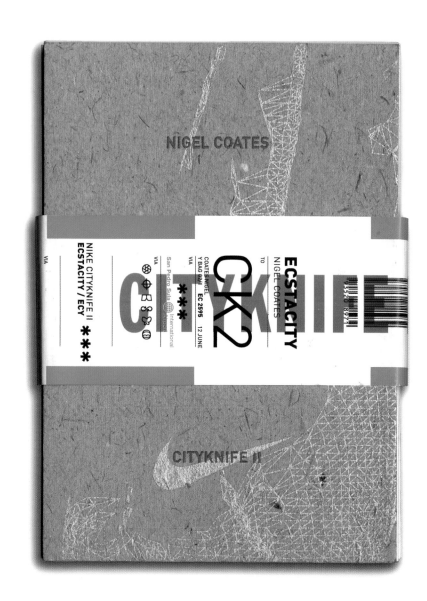

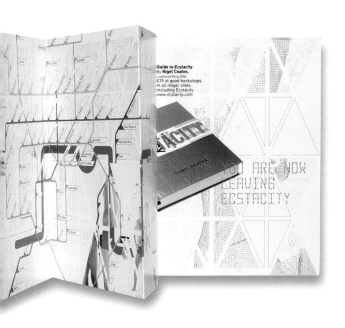

Art Director:
Justus Oehler
Designers:
Justus Oehler,
Josephine Rank
Client:
Mozarthaus Vienna
Software:
QuarkXPress
Paper/Materials:
Munken Lynx

BOCCALATTE
**C Town Bling
Catalog**

154

Art Director:
Suzanne Boccalatte
Client:
Campbelltown Arts
Centre
Software:
Adobe Creative Suite
Paper/Materials:
Monza Foil Stamp

mattress is a threshold to sleep upon /
a strange quilted force / of softening
matters / and everlasting springs /
a cushion for the body's travels through
the times of night / at whichever
hour / off the ground / off the floor /
a place for yonder life / an island
for refuge and panic and trauma and
fatigue / a site of unimagined grief and
imagined love / a thing / an artful
object for flesh and blood and thought
to spread like animals / adrift / falling
from nowhere in divine-particular /
just here / this moment / falling into
rage or calm / eyes closed and seeing /
infinite operas / wondrous vistas /
delicate gifts subtle dangers embracing
voids / dying for hours / or maybe not /
instead / wide-awake / nerve ends
razor-sharp / feverish / the ill or joyful
creature gushes leaks seeps moults
rubs squeezes / leaving itself like a
ghost on the surface and more ghostly
still below the surface / on the mythical
heart of the thing's patience / its exact
presence / weight depth length width /
the body descends willingly / becomes
threshold too / abandoning its own
heart-dream / each laboured mattress
made of earth substances pulled to
light / for unprecedented passioned and
dispassioned touches / the mattress-
cosmos awaits something-to-come / and
it does / birth / death / and every minute
betwixt state / even now at this late
hour / an image of it / refuge as refuse /
excessive in its worn broken luxuriance /
a desert / deserted / recorded /
presented / simply saying 'I am'

VOICE
Photographic
Exhibition **C**atalog

155

Art Director:
Scott Carslake
Designer:
Scott Carslake
Client:
Toby Richardson
Software:
Adobe InDesign,
Photoshop
Paper/Materials:
Paper by Daltons,
Process Color, Saddle
Stitch

Teresa's story
'We miss our mother'
Nkwazi compound
Ndola, Zambia

Teresa died on 8 May 2001,
just three months after this
photograph was taken for
Cold Heaven. Her two
children, Aaron and Mavis,
were ten and eight years
old. They still cry at night.

'We miss our mother,' Aaron
says quietly. 'She looked
after us and brought us food
and clothes. When she was
ill, we swept the house,
washed the clothes and
fetched water. We liked
looking after her because
she was our mother.'

When Don McCullin gave
Aaron this photograph,
he turned away, overcome,
his face in his hands. Aaron
had never seen a photograph
of his mother. Today it
stands framed, in pride
of place, on the dresser.

'I am sure Aaron has had
dreams of his mother,' said
McCullin. 'He must have
thought for a second that he
had been living a nightmare
for the past three years and
that she was actually there
when he saw that photo.'

The children are lucky to
have found a loving and
secure home with their
paternal grandparents,
Margaret, 62, and Oleshi,
69. The children's father,
their only son, died of an
HIV-related disease in 2001.

On the day McCullin arrived,
they were eating leftover
grains of dried maize for
breakfast. Oleshi earns
40 pence/80 cents a day as
a cobbler. The family cannot
afford the Zambian staple
of maize porridge. Although
a community organisation
pays for the children's
schooling, the family has
to pay for the water the
children collect from a
standpipe each day; water
services are prioritised in
Zambia. Often they go to
bed hungry.

'But we are happy, praise
the Lord,' says Margaret.
'We have lost our only
son and now we have
the grandchildren to
replace him.'

'When I look at Teresa's picture she comes across as strangely beautiful and quietly courageous – a woman who could barely move and yet was bringing up two children.'

Don McCullin

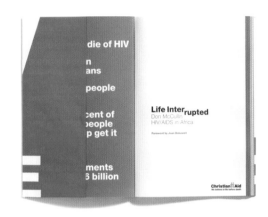

LIPPA PEARCE
**"Life Interrupted"
Catalog for Don
McCulin Exhibition**

156

Art Director:
Harry Pearce
Designer:
Harry Pearce
Client:
Christian Aid

Art Director:
Angus Hyland
Client:
Parker Pens

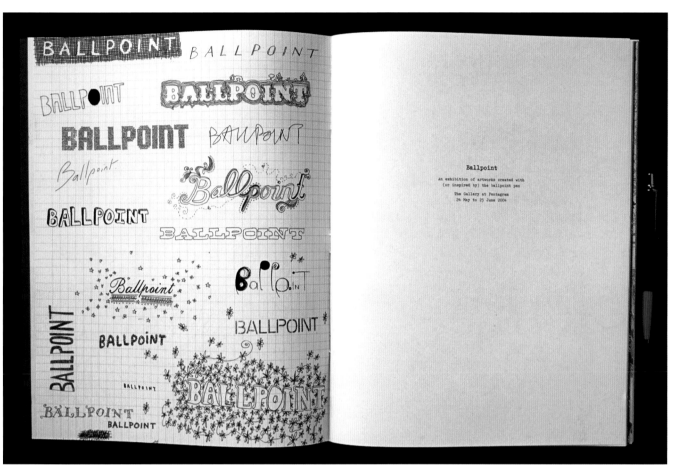

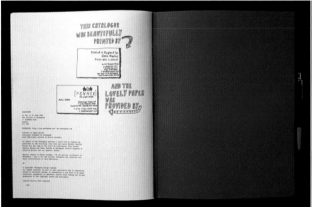

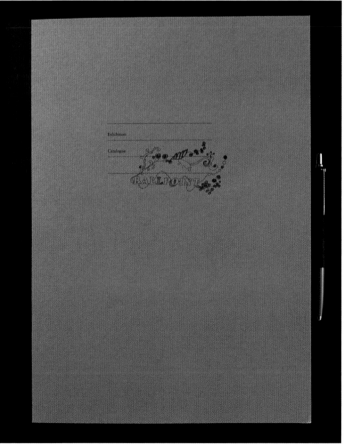

The RSA's House

ATELIER WORKS
RSA House Guide

158

Art Director:
Ian Chilvers
Designer:
Ian Chilvers
Client:
Royal Society of Arts
Software:
QuarkXPress

Art Director:
Experimental Jetset
Designer:
Experimental Jetset
Client:
De Theater Compagne

SELF
PROMOTION

RED DESIGN

160

ALLEGRO 168

161

HAT-TRICK
DESIGN

162

TOGETHER
DESIGN

163

TIMESPIN

164

PRIME
CREATIVE LTD

165

BOB DINETZ
DESIGN

166

SÄGENVIER
DESIGN KOM-
MUNIKATION

167

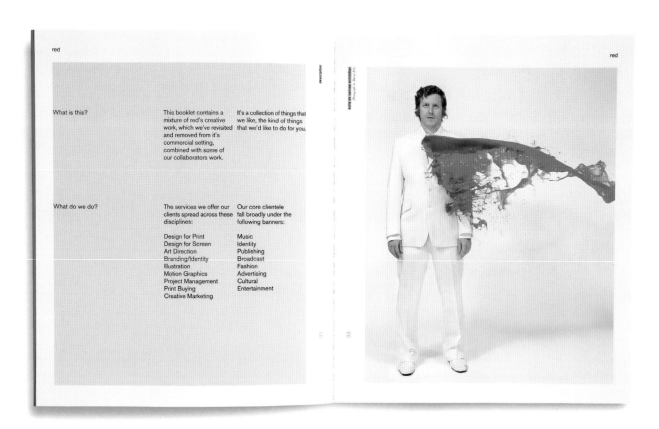

**Red Design + Art
Direction**

160

Art Director:
Red Design
Designer:
Red Design
Client:
Red Design
Software:
Freehand,
Adobe Photoshop,
QuarkXPress
Paper/Materials:
Fedrigoni White,
Satimat

red
design +
art direction

still.
moving.
interactive.

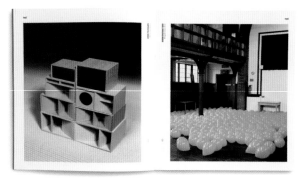

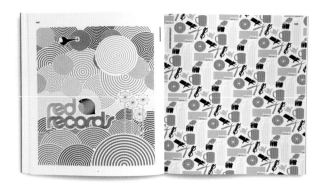

ALLEGRO 168
**12th Anniversary
Carnival Invitation**

161

Art Directors:
Nicole Vallée,
Mario L'Écuyer
Designer:
Mario L'Écuyer
Client:
Allegro 168
Software:
QuarkXPress,
Adobe Illustrator,
Adobe Photoshop
Paper/Materials:
Fraser Papers
Pegasus, Kraft
paper bags, custom
rubber stamp

HAT-TRICK DESIGN
How Do You Do?
Self-Promotional
Brochure
162

Art Directors:
Jim Sutherland,
Gareth Howat,
David Kimpton
Designers:
Jim Sutherland,
Adam Giles,
Ben Christie
Client:
Hat-Trick Design
Software:
QuarkXPress
Paper/Materials:
Astralux, Lite Gloss,
Hanno Gloss

The 'N' becomes a window into a myriad of images that demonstrate the diversity, brightness, excitement and scale of the natural world.

Under the new identity, there is no doubt that anything produced by the Natural History Museum signifies a distinct and powerful experience, courtesy of a distinct and powerful source: nature itself.

355 pairs of legs

12 metres long

Over 100 k

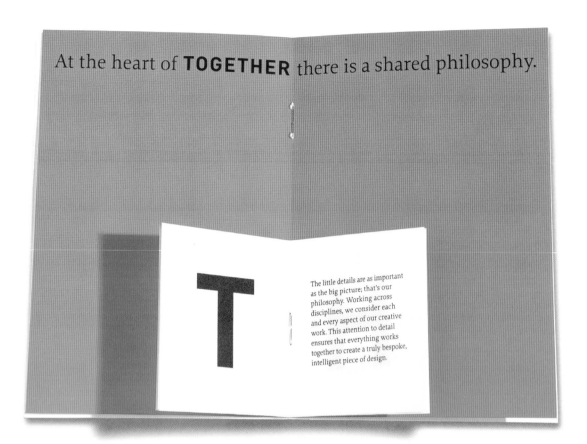

At the heart of **TOGETHER** there is a shared philosophy.

TOGETHER DESIGN
Self-Promotional Brochure

163

Designers:
Katja Thielen,
Heidi Lightfoot
Client:
Together Design
Software:
QuarkXPress
Paper|Materials:
Conqueror Wove,
Metallic Foil Block

The little details are as important as the big picture; that's our philosophy. Working across disciplines, we consider each and every aspect of our creative work. This attention to detail ensures that everything works together to create a truly bespoke, intelligent piece of design.

TOGETHER

GALLERY
of COSTUME
& TEXTILES

WE LIKE BEAUTIFUL THINGS

When Kyra Segal approached us with a view to creating an identity for her eponymous clothing collection, we jumped at the chance. Beautifully designed and impeccably crafted, her pieces are inspired by the timeless aesthetics and craftsmanship of the archives at The Gallery of Costume and Textiles, the famous emporium of antique textiles and vintage clothes founded by Kyra's father Lionel. Our challenge was to create an identity to be applied across the retail environment, which would tell the story of the collection's provenance and aesthetics, yet stand alone as a modern, covetable brand.

We found inspiration for the identity in the phoenix, a symbol of resurrection, good luck, and a theme of great personal resonance to Kyra herself. Depicted in an antique, chinoiserie style, the identity ultimately reflects the eclectic nature of the Gallery and of Kyra's own aesthetic, as well as being a beautiful thing in itself.

WE LIKE FINDING REASONS TO CELEBRATE

Which is why we were only too keen to work on a project which would set the corks a-popping on a regular basis. Katja from Together comes from a wine-making family in the Mosel valley, and the time was right to introduce their wines to the UK market. With no retail presence and a largely word-of-mouth approach to marketing, they needed a website to support their all-important ordering system, as well as a redesigned logo for bottle labels, tags, postcards and wine corks.

We developed a new logo and commissioned illustrations which became the backbone of the website. Taking the form of a conversation, the site features both real and fictitious characters taking the visitor on a tour of the Thielen wine cellar, and engagingly holding forth about the wines, and the history, philosophy and techniques behind them. The creative work has a look, feel and tone which is refreshingly different and unique, which may reflect the fact that most of the contributors were paid in wine, a good deal of it in advance, for inspiration's sake. www.thielenwine.com

Art Directors:
Tino Schmidt,
Robert Berneis
Designer:
Tino Schmidt
Client:
Timespin
Software:
Adobe InDesign
Paper/Materials:
Galaxy Keramik,
transparent paper
with metallic color
varnished print

PRIME CREATIVE
LTD
**Self-Promotional
Book**
165

Art Director:
Sue Fearnsides
Designers:
Craig Hardaker,
Adam Kenyon,
Chris Taylor
Client:
Prime Creative Ltd
Software:
QuarkXPress,
Adobe Photoshop,
Freehand
Paper/Materials:
Amadeus Silk 350 and
200 gsm

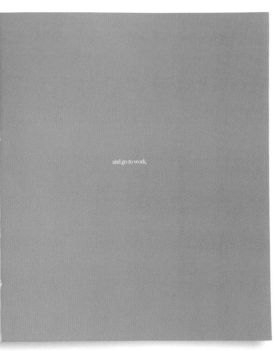

decide what you want, decide what you are willing to change. establish your priorities

and go to work.

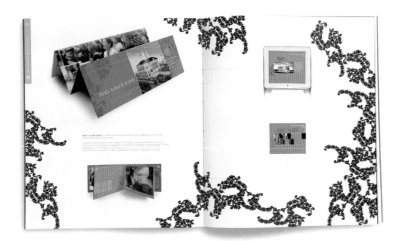

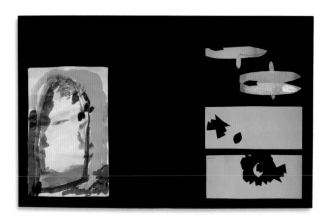

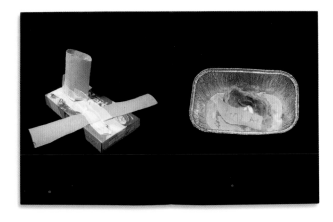

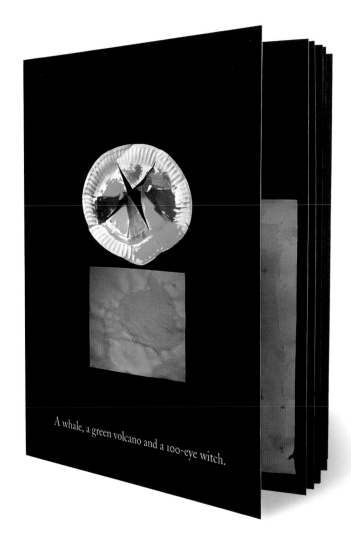

A whale, a green volcano and a 100-eye witch.

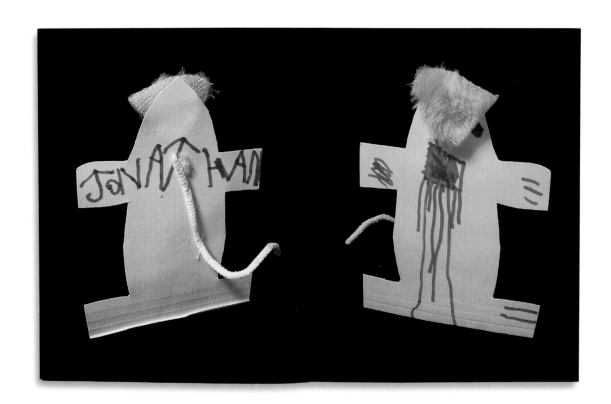

BOB DINETZ
DESIGN
100 Eye Witch

166

Designer:
Bob Dinetz
Client:
Bob Dinetz Design
Software:
Adobe Photoshop,
QuarkXPress
Paper/Materials:
80 lb uncoated book

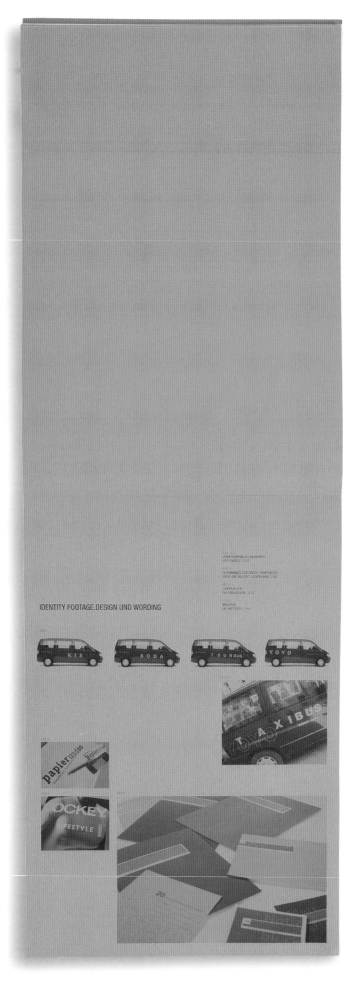

IDENTITY FOOTAGE.DESIGN UND WORDING

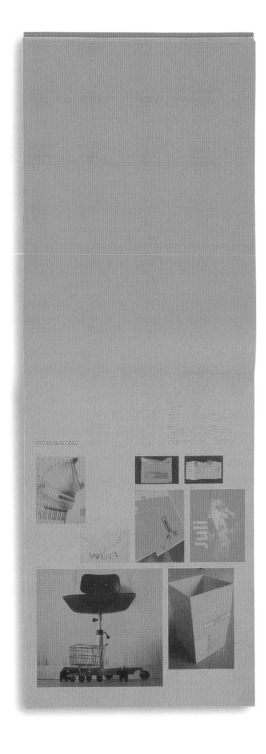

ERSCHEINUNGSBILD

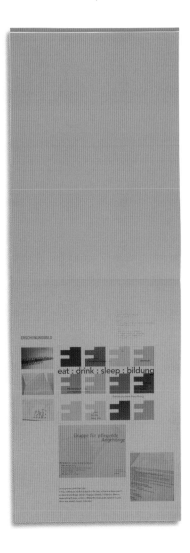

SÄGENVIER DESIGN
KOMMUNIKATION
**Gute Gestaltung
Miteinander**

167

Art Director:
Sigi Ramoser
Designers:
Klaus Österle,
Sabine Sowieja
Client:
Sägenvier
Paper/Materials:
Brotop

EDUCATIONAL AND
NONPROFIT

Daedalus Edition

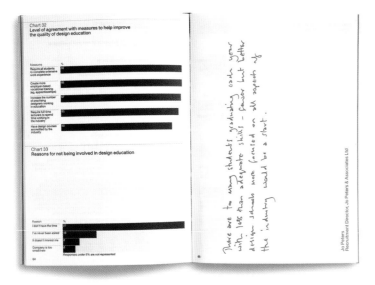

CARTLIDGE LEVENE
The Business of Design, Design Industry Research
168

Art Director:
Ian Cartlidge
Designer:
Cartlidge Levene
Client:
Design Council
Software:
Adobe InDesign
Paper/Materials:
Howard Smith (cover),
Think White (text),
McNaughton
Cyclus (text)

HAT-TRICK DESIGN
The Salvation Army International Head-quarters Brochure
169

Art Director:
David Kimpton
Designer:
Ben Christie
Client:
The Salvation Army
Software:
QuarkXPress
Paper/Materials:
Bible Paper

The Co-Chairmen and
Committee of The Magic
Britannia would like to do all
they can to keep the running costs
as low as possible. Throughout the
year, during the maximum funds raised
that we can work to maintain and
develop, the greater impact our
work is central to achieving this
is the generosity and support we
receive from so many individuals
and companies – from the printing
of this programme by Fulmar
Colour Printing to the design work
by Iana. From the donation of the
resources, time and raffle prizes
to the time and effort that so many of our
team who volunteer, magicians and
performers. Each one vital to
achieving our objectives.

**THANK YOU
TO ALL OF OUR
SUPPORTERS**

DOMESTIC LABOUR ENFORCED IN PERU

Anti-Slavery is committed
to eliminating all forms
of slavery in today's world.
Slavery, servitude and forced
labour are violations of individual
freedom, which deny basic dignity
and fundamental human rights.
Anti-Slavery supports today's
fight for tomorrow's freedom by
exposing current cases of slavery
and campaigning for their
eradication, supporting the
initiatives of local organisations
to release people, supporting the
prevention and rehabilitation
of child domestic workers,
and pressing for more effective
implementation of international
laws against slavery.

**David Simpson
Honorary Life Member,
Anti-Slavery International**

**ANTI-SLAVERY
INTERNATIONAL'S
MISSION**

INARIA
Colors of the World

170

Art Directors:
Andrew Thomas,
Debora Berardi
Designers:
Andrew Thomas,
Debora Berardi
Client:
Anti-Slavery
International
Paper/Materials:
Hanno Art Silk
200 gsm (text),
Hanno Art Gloss
320 gsm (cover)

POULIN + MORRIS INC.
Brooklyn Botanic Garden, Master Plan

171

Designers:
L. Richard Poulin,
Anna Crider
Client:
Brooklyn Botanic
Garden
Software:
Adobe InDesign
Paper/Materials:
Sappi, Lustro Dull

HVAD
Art School Exhibition Brochure
172

Art Director:
Henk van Assen
Designer:
Henk van Assen
Client:
Yale University
School of Art
Software:
Adobe InDesign
Paper/Materials:
Printer Stock
uncoated

DIE SCHWEIZ IST EIN SCHÖNES LAND
SWITZERLAND IS A BEAUTIFUL COUNTRY

Die Schweiz ist ein schönes Land. Sie hier vorzustellen ist schwierig, zu knapp bemessen ist der Platz, aber dies spielt eigentlich keine Rolle – ihr werdet eure Schweiz selber entdecken, kennen, schätzen, lieben lernen. Oder auch hassen. So verschieden die Menschen, so verschieden die Wahrnehmungen, Erlebnisse, Eindrücke – und zu behaupten, dass jede und jeder von der Schweiz begeistert sein würde wäre unverantwortlich. Lasst euch offen auf sie ein – und die Chancen auf einen friedlichen, formenden, fordernden Aufenthalt sind gross.

Gleich vorweg sei euch eine Angst genommen – man sagt den Schweizern und Schweizerinnen nach, sie seinen „verschlossen". Ihr werdet zum Glück nie „die Schweizerin" und „den Schweizer" treffen – die gibt es nicht. Und somit erübrigt es sich auch darüber nachzudenken, ob sie nun verschlossen sind oder nicht. Klar, es gibt Mentalitäten, Bräuche, Traditionen. Zum Beispiel macht man in Zürich, in der Schweiz allgemein weniger Spontanbesuche, dafür macht man etwas ab und hat dann auch Zeit, trifft sich zum Essen zu Hause, in gemütlichem Kreis. Und denkt daran wo ihr steht – viel weniger „in der Schweiz" als „an der hgkz in Zürich" – dieses Umfeld wird euch prägen, tragen oder fallen lassen, nicht „die Schweiz". Sogar von offizieller Stelle wurde deren Nichtexistenz bestätigt, "La Suisse n'existe pas", das Motto für die Weltausstellung in Sevilla, 1992. Das gilt auch heute noch, ganz im Einklang mit den Zeiträumen, in denen sich in der Schweiz etwas zu bewegen pflegt. Und genau das ist der richtige Geist: die Schweiz gibt es nicht – ihr müsst sie euch erschaffen, ihr, die ihr von aussen kommt. Ihr müsst sie und euch in ihr erschaffen.

Switzerland is a beautiful country. It is difficult to describe the country here because there is not enough space; however this does not really matter because you will discover, get to know, appreciate, and learn to love Switzerland by yourself. Or maybe even hate it. As different as people are, each has different opinions, experiences, impressions; to assume that everyone will love Switzerland is simply irresponsible. Be open in your approach to Switzerland and then the chances of a happy, formative and demanding stay are great.

To begin with, let us remove one fear: it is said that the Swiss are "reserved". You will never come across "the typical Swiss person", that person simply doesn't exist. And thus it isn't even necessary to think about whether they are reserved or not. Of course, there are different mentalities, customs, and traditions. For example, people in Zurich and in Switzerland in general, don't visit spontaneously as people in other countries might do. However, they arrange to meet friends for a meal at home, taking their time about it in a more intimate circle. And remember where you are: not so much "in Switzerland" as "at the hgkz in Zurich". This is the environment that will influence you, support you or drop you, but not "Switzerland". Its non-existence has even been verified at the official level: "La Suisse n'existe pas" was the slogan for the World Exhibition in Seville in 1992. This still applies today, in line with the periods in which Switzerland was accustomed to get things moving. And that is just the right attitude: Switzerland doesn't exist – you must create your own Switzerland, you who have arrived from another country. You must create her for yourself, and yourself within her.

WER/WHO: Magda Stanová ◾ WOHER/FROM: Tatranská Lomnica, Slowakei
STUDIENBEREICH/DEPARTMENT: SBK

UNFOLDED
School of Art and Design, Zurich, International Reader

173

Art Director:
Friedrich-Wilhem Graf
Creative Director:
Nadia Gisler
Photography:
Stefan Burger
Client:
School of Art and Design, Zurich, International Office
Software:
Adobe InDesign, Adobe Photoshop, Adobe Illustrator OSX
Paper/Materials:
Munken Pure Paper

HGKZ DEPARTEMENTE
HGKZ DEPARTMENTS

Interactive Media: Die Studierenden erwerben sich professionelle Kenntnisse im Umgang mit neuesten Medientechnologien. Dieser Begriff erweitert wie um akustische und taktile Dimensionen und erstrecken sich über den Studienbereich Gestaltung, Game Design, Studierende, Dozierende sowie Gastexperten arbeiten zusammen in einer Labor-/Atelieratmosphäre um «space»-time of possibility», in dem Prozessorientierung und Experiment gleichermassen von Bedeutung sind.

http://interactive.hgkz.ch

SCENOGRAPHICAL DESIGN
Der Studienschwerpunkt Scenographical Design (SGD) fokussiert auf die Konzipierung und Realisierung narrativer und gestalterischer Gesamtwerke, wobei die szenografische Raum ins Zentrum steht: sei es makro, makro, real, virtuell, urban, kommerziell, museal oder theatral. Der Studien ist durch zwei Entwicklungsstränge gekennzeichnet, die auf jeder Ebene der Ausbildung miteinander in Beziehung stehen wie die zwei Seiten einer Medaille: die Exhibiting Arts (ausstellende Künste) und die Performing Arts (darstellende Künste). Im Scenographical Design werden narrative Environments in Zusammenarbeit mit gut inszenierten wohlinszenierten Dramaturgie. Dies setzt einen Scenographical Designer voraus, der als unabhängiger und beweglicher Denker in der Lage ist, szenografische Prozesse kognitiv und intuitiv zu steuern. Den Studierenden werden vier Vertiefungsrichtungen angeboten: Urban Space, Cyberspace, Exhibition Space, Theatre Space.

STYLE & DESIGN
Der Studienschwerpunkt Style & Design (StD) pflegt an Sinne einer Trendlabors die Auseinandersetzung mit inhaltlich und gesellschaftlich relevanten Erschei-

Interactive Media: students acquire professional knowledge in using the latest media technologies. This concept is expanded to include its auditory and tactile dimensions, producing concepts and solutions in the arts of interactive design together with the students. Game Design: students, lecturers and guest experts work together in a laboratory/studio atmosphere to create a «space»-time of possibility» in which process orientation and experiment take on equal importance.

http://interactive.hgkz.ch

SCENOGRAPHICAL DESIGN
The special field Scenographical Design (SGD) focuses on the formulation and implementation of complex works of narrative and design in which the scenographical environment is of central importance, whether this be at the micro-, macro-, real, virtual, urban, commercial, museum-related or theatrical level. The course features two development strands which stand in close relationship to each other at all stages of instruction like the two sides of a coin: the exhibiting arts and the performing arts.
In Scenographical Design, narrative environments are created with well-integrated dramatic technique. This presupposes a designer able to control scenographical processes cognitively and intuitively in an independent and agile thinker. Students are offered four special areas: urban space, cyberspace, exhibition space and theatre space.

http://sgd.hgkz.ch

STYLE & DESIGN
The special field Style & Design (StD) concentrates on investigating aesthetically and socially relevant renewal fixtures in the sense of laboratory work in trend analysis. The main emphasis lies in the observation and analysis of trends, style movements/style history, sources and communities and their implementation and

you can hear it in the **voices** of the students...

Harvard Business School is a community of people engaged in many activities focused on one purpose—developing leaders.

STOLTZE DESIGN
Harvard Business School Admissions Brochure
174

Art Director:
Clifford Stoltze
Designer:
Roy Burns
Client:
Harvard Business School
Software:
QuarkXPress
Paper/Materials:
Finch Fine

KOLEGRAM
**Canadian Archive
Association
Promotion**
175

Designer:
Gontran Blais
Client:
Library & Archives
Canada
Paper/Materials:
Domtar Titanium and
Proterra

RB-M

**Camberwell &
Chelsea Short
Courses Brochure**

176

Art Director:
Richard
Bonner-Morgan
Designer:
Richard
Bonner-Morgan
Photographer:
Richard Learoyd
Client:
London Artscom
Limited
Software:
QuarkXPress
Paper/Materials:
Nimrod Silk

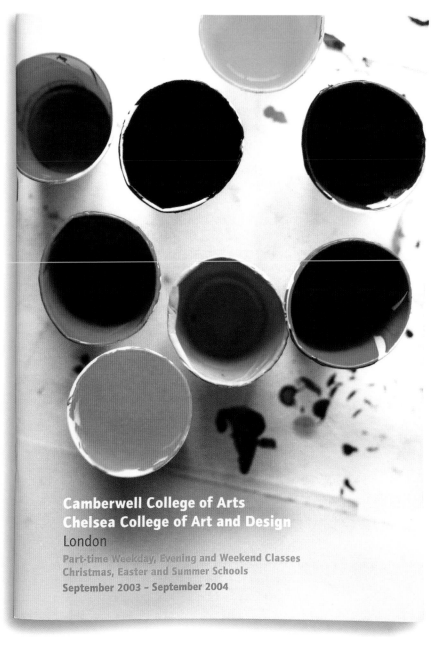

**Camberwell College of Arts
Chelsea College of Art and Design**
London
Part-time Weekday, Evening and Weekend Classes
Christmas, Easter and Summer Schools
September 2003 – September 2004

Charrette 2
Communities in the Greenbelt: Visionary Social
and Environmental Proposals (Access and Activity)

Charrette 1
Access to the Riverfront at Purfleet

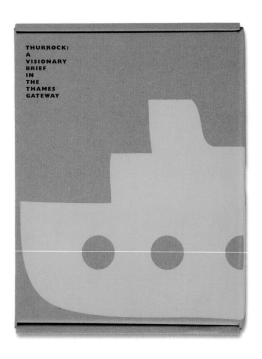

THURROCK:
A
VISIONARY
BRIEF
IN
THE
THAMES
GATEWAY

KERR/NOBLE
**A Visionary Brief
in the Thames
Gateway**
177

Art Director:
Kerr/Noble
Designer:
Kerr/Noble
Client:
General Public
Agency

Contents

Introduction

International Case Studies

Notes

Atlas

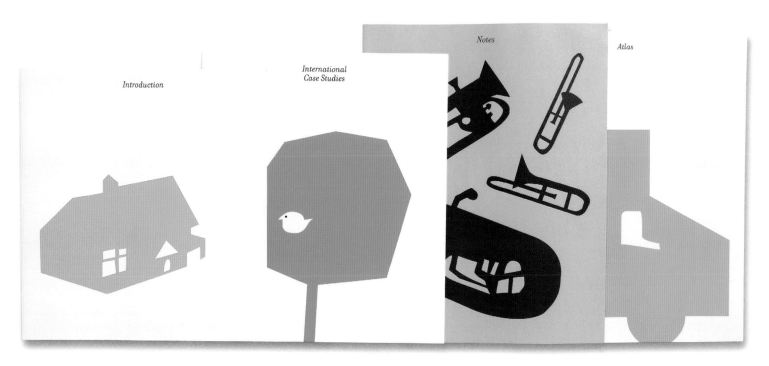

4. KEY CHALLENGES. In the next fifteen years Thurrock will face many changes: **1.** A self-generated population increase of around 7% (10,000 people) but a potential incoming population of twice this number. **2.** Up to 17,000 new homes, densifying existing neighbourhoods but also creating new communities. **3.** Economic restructuring and a need for a vastly more skilled workforce. **4.** A major economic attractor in the new Shell Haven port which will be one of Europe's largest deep-water facilities. **5.** A new emphasis on sustainable waste management with the closure of the major landfill sites. **6.** The increasing threat of flooding, with high water levels becoming normal rather than rare.

PENTAGRAM DESIGN, SAN FRANCISCO
San Francisco Botanical Garden
178

Art Director:
Kit Hinrichs
Designers:
Belle How,
Jessica Siegel
Client:
The San Francisco
Botanical Garden
Association
Software:
Adobe InDesign

Think about what makes a city great: Is it the spirit and outlook of its people? Its geography? Its history? San Francisco, a great city by any measure, has it all — including one inspiring resource no great city should be without: a botanical garden where people can experience nature, learn about plants and the environment, relax, and seek respite from urban life. Since 1940, San Francisco Botanical Garden at Strybing Arboretum has embodied all that makes San Francisco great — a jewel-like setting, a mild climate in which diversity thrives, a conservation spirit, and a sensibility that cherishes beauty and seeks to share it with others. For the people of the Bay Area, this unique garden is more than a place in Golden Gate Park. It's a place in our hearts, a familiar backdrop for the times of our lives. On its daisy-dotted meadows, we've picnicked or sat sketching a magnificent magnolia in bloom. On its meandering paths, we've contemplated life's big issues, answered a child's questions about nature, or sought inspiration for a home garden, even if it's a window box. However we experience it, this garden reminds us that connecting with and protecting nature — whether we're dedicated gardeners or just admirers of Earth's diverse beauty — makes us more alive. For 50 years, the Botanical Garden Society has augmented public funding to make San Francisco Botanical Garden great. Now, with your help, we can turn San Francisco's garden — the garden we love — into one of the world's finest botanical gardens. This opportunity is unique and perishable, and the time to seize it is now, while we have a vision of what our great city's garden can become and the talented team to bring that vision to life.

SÄGENVIER DESIGN
KOMMUNIKATION
Attention
Schulden Falle

179

Art Director:
Sigi Ramoser
Designers:
Klaus Österle,
Oli Ruhm,
Silvia Keckeis
Client:
AK Vorarlberg

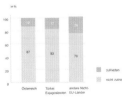

'I was attracted by the one-year programme and the opportunity to experience French and Asian culture. In a world that continues to get closer, INSEAD stands out as an example of how students and faculty drawn from across the globe can come together to make an unforgettable experience. When I came to INSEAD a year ago, I never expected to leave with the diversity and depth of friendships I have today'. **Monisha Dillon, 25 (United Kingdom)**

'I chose INSEAD because of the diversity of the student body. I had good friends who were alums who spoke highly of the place. Also, I had met their friends and felt they were broadminded and internationally orientated. The ability to move geographies and, at my relatively mature age, the one year programme, also appealed to me. It was a good choice exceeding my expectations'. **Saman Ahsani, 31 (Iran)**

NB:STUDIO
Insead
MBA Program

180

Art Directors:
Nick Finney, Ben Stott,
Alan Dye
Designer:
Daniel Lock
Client:
Insead

One year to earn your place among our alumni.

In a sense, you never leave INSEAD. As your MBA programme comes to an end, your life as an INSEAD alumnus begins. It is likely to be an exciting, exciting life. You will join a diverse alumni network of around 32,200 members, 15,300 from the MBA programme and 16,900 from Executive programmes.

Our alumni live and work in over 150 countries across all continents. They may be geographically diverse, but they share the same entrepreneurial streak. Twenty years after gaining their MBA, over 40% of our alumni own and manage their own business. The advice and encouragement that flows between INSEAD alumni is an important tool in this business-building.

You may well wish to remain in touch with INSEAD. A thousand alumni volunteers sit on national alumni association committees, helping to organise reunions and international speaking events as well as interviewing MBA candidates in their home countries. Two alumni share their views here.

34/35

Patricia Sharma-Inglis MBA '99
Head of Marketing, Standard
Chartered Bank Singapore

'I was previously a strategy consultant with US firm Bain & Company so business school was a given. INSEAD was a host obvious choice than a US school, but it was the best decision I ever made. INSEAD taught me a lot about business and most still about life. It gave me a fantastic network of alumni contacts and launched my professional career.'

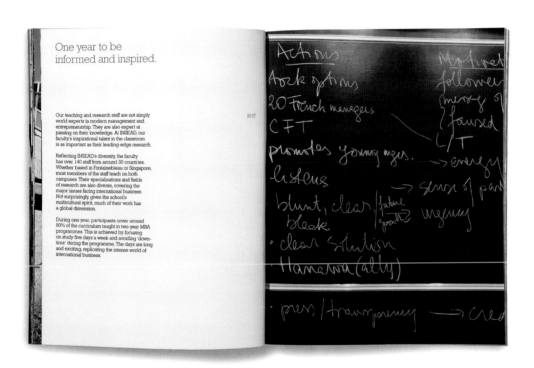

One year to be informed and inspired.

Our teaching and research staff are not simply world experts in modern management and entrepreneurship. They are also expert at passing on their knowledge. At INSEAD, our faculty's inspirational talent in the classroom is as important as their leading-edge research.

Reflecting INSEAD's diversity, the faculty has over 140 staff from around 30 countries. Whether based in Fontainebleau or Singapore, most members of the staff teach on both campuses. Their specialisations and fields of research are also diverse, covering the major issues facing international business. Not surprisingly, given the school's multicultural spirit, much of their work has a global dimension.

During one year, participants cover around 80% of the curriculum taught in two-year MBA programmes. This is achieved by focusing on study five days a week and avoiding 'down-time' during the programme. The days are long and exciting, replicating the intense world of international business.

16/17

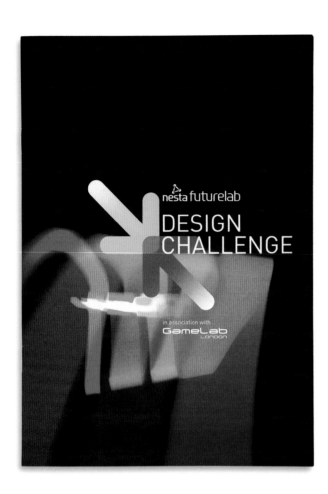

Client:
Nesta
Software:
Freehand MX

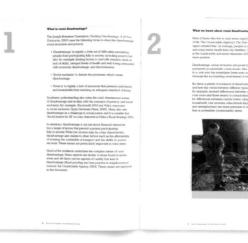

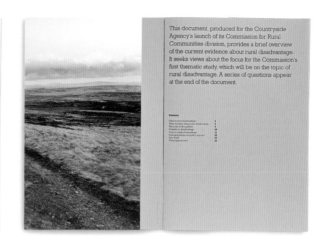

MYTTON WILLIAMS
**Rural
Disadvantage
Study Brochure**
182

Art Director:
Bob Mytton
Designer:
Matt Judge
Client:
Commission for Rural
Communities
Software:
Adobe InDesign
Paper/Materials:
Revive Silk

Building the Jubilee School
Everyone and the Architect

Building Sights
Building Sights is a campaign to involve the public in building projects. Run by Arts Council England and the Commission for Architecture and the Built Environment (CABE), Building Sights is an award scheme to celebrate the best examples of public involvement and a website that provides practical information and ideas about how to go about it.

This book is the story of a new school in Tulse Hill, Brixton, London. It comes in two parts;

Part One
How the process was shared

Part Two
How the school was designed

Awards for the school

Aug 2001
RSA Art for Architecture Award

Aug 2003
RIBA Regional Award

Sept 2003
Short-listed for the Prime Minister's Better Public Building Award

Sept 2003
Short-listed for a Building Construction Industry Award

Part One
A guide to sharing the process – getting everyone involved in the process of creating a new building.

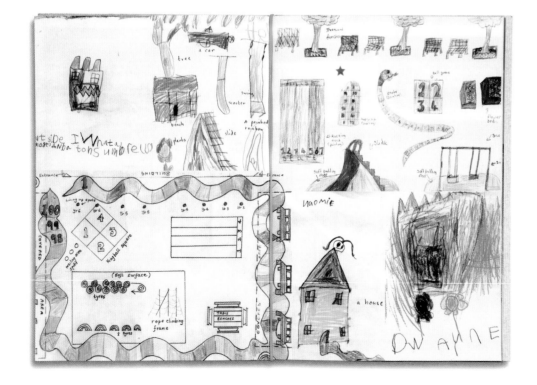

STUDIO
MYERSCOUGH
Jubilee

183

Art Director:
Morag Myerscough
Designers:
Morag Myerscough,
David Lowbridge
Client:
Arts Council England,
CABE & Allford, Hall,
Monaghan, Morris

How the process was shared

Why bother?

An important development in architecture over the last few years has been a desire to include people in the process of making new buildings. This has resulted from a more informed and engaged community wanting to have an input and to connect with the people responsible for making their built environment.

Architects, planners, clients and local councils are themselves keen to share the excitement of building and to learn by sharing this process with a wide audience.

With any new building it makes sense to involve and inform a wide public about the project long before it is actually finished – it helps create feelings of ownership and starts to build a relationship with the building – its future uses and place within the community.

Some ideas about how to do it

The design and construction process is an amazing and fascinating system – of ideas, dreams, materials, people, machines and money.

Every time a building is built it is a small miracle and there are many ways to let people be part of this event and everyone involved in the project has a part to play.

The Jubilee School project was shared through;
– community awareness
– building construction awareness
– site access/site tours
– communication and events

The process of designing this new school was about creating a great new building for the children and community of this part of Brixton – and doing it through creativity, openess and collaboration.

Building the Jubilee School Everyone and the Architect

Allford Hall Monaghan Morris

www.buildingsights.org.uk

netball
football
basketball

skip
map
site
stre

AGENCY DIRECTORY

057, 074
300million
1 Rosoman Place
London EC1R OJY
UK
T. 020.7833.3898
F. 020.7833.1888
nigel@300million.com

161
Allegro 168
150 Cathcart Street
Ottawa, Ontario K1N 5B8
Canada
T. 613.789.7168
F. 613.789.4168
nvallee@allegro.ca

076, 079
Aloof Design
5 Fisher Street
Lewes, East Sussex
BN7 2DG
UK
T 01273.470887
michelle@aloofdesign.com

004, 087, 091, 138, 139, 158
Atelier Works
The Old Piano Factory, 5
Charlton Kings Road
London NW5 2SB
UK
T. 0207.284.2215
F. 0207.284.2242
john@atelierworks.co.uk

055, 124
BBK Studio
648 Monroe NW, Suite 212
Grand Rapids, MI 49503
USA
T. 616.459.4444
F. 616.459.4477
yang@bbkstudio.com

126
bc, mh, James Lambert
32 Sunbury Workshops
Swanfield Street
London E2 7LF
UK
T. 020.7739.2917
email@bcmh.co.uk

008, 125
**Billy Blue Creative
Precinct**
PO Box 728
North Sydney,
NSW 2059
Australia
T. 61.2.94923257
F. 61.2. 99559577
justin@billyblue.com.au

065, 068, 070
Blok Design
Sombrerete 515#,
Hipdromo La Condesa
Mexico DF
06170
Mexico
T. 5255.5515.2423
blokdesign@att.net.mx

015, 119
Blue River
The Foundry, Forth Banks
New Castle Upon Tyne
NE1 3PA
UK
T. 0191.261.0000
F. 0191.261.0010
design@blueriver.co.uk

166
Bob Dinetz Design
236 Bonita Avenue
Piedmont, CA 94611
USA
T. 415.606.6792
bob@bobdinetzdesign.com

154
Boccalatte
Studio 43.61 Marlborough
St., Surry Hills
Sydney, NSW 2010
Australia
T. 612.93104149
F. 612.93104149
cheri@boccalatte.com

075
Brunazzi & Associati
22 Via Andorno
Torino, 10153
Italy
T. 011.8125.397
F. 011.8170.702
info@brunazzi.com

045
Bungee Associates
804A North Bridge Road
Singapore
Singapore
T. 65.62995983
F. 65.62995973
joe@bungeeassociates.com

121
Burgeff Design
Tecualiapan 36
Mexico City
Mexico
T. 5255.5554.5931
diseno@burgeff.com

039
CSAA Creative Services
100 Van Ness Avenue
San Francisco, CA 94102
USA
T. 451.934.3556
F. 415.701.8431
julie_keenan@csaa.com

005, 009, 011, 019, 028, 035,
077, 082
Cahan & Associates
171 2nd Street, 5th Floor
San Francisco, CA 94105
USA
T. 415.621.0915
F. 415.621.7642
info@cahanassociates.com

025
Carré Noir Roma
Via Tata Giovanni, 8
00154 Roma
Italy
T. 39.06570201
F. 39.065745708
msagrati@katamail.com /
massimiliano.sagrati
@carrenoir-roma.it

041, 116, 168
Cartlidge Levene
238 St. John Street
London EC1V 40H
UK
T. 020.7251.6608
F. 020.7253.0804
info@cartlidgelevene.co.uk

081
**Cem Erutku Tasarim
Studyosu - C375**
Tarik Zafer Tunayasok
3/6 Gunussuyu
Istanbul
Turkey
T. 212.2497709
F. 212.2497746
cerutku@c375.com

007
The Chase
1 North Parade,
Parsonage Gardens
Manchester M3 2NH
UK
T. 0161.832.5575
F. 0161.832.5567
emma.cotsford@thechase.
co.uk

115, 140
Cheng Design
2433 E Aloha Street
Seattle, WA 98112
USA
T. 206.328.4047
F. 206.685.1657
kcheng@u.washington.edu

062, 067, 130
Design Project
Round Foundry Media
Centre
Unit G15, Foundry Street
Leeds LS11 5QP
UK
T. 0870.420.2422
enquiries@designproject.
co.uk

018
Doppio Design
Suite 1.15, 22-36 Mountain
Street, Ultimo
Sydney, NSW 2007
Australia
T. 61.2.9212.0405
F. 61.2.6280.2457
studio@doppiodesign.com

085, 103
**Dowling Design & Art
Direction**
Navigation House
48 Millgate
Newark NG24 4TS
UK
T. 01636.612012
F. 01636.612058
john@dowlingdesign.com

121
ELECO
Tecualiapan 36 VII/8
Mexico City
Mexico
T. 55.55545931
F. 55.55545931
diseno@burgeff.com

086, 093, 142, 159
Experimental Jetset
Jan Hanzenstraat 37
1st Floor
1053 SK Amsterdam
Netherlands
T. 20.4686036
F. 20.4686037
info@jetset.nl

128, 129
FanClubProject
Kartuizersstraat 19
1000 Brussels
Belgium
T. 0032.2.289.5918
F. 0032.2.502.5959
sander@fanclubproject.com

090, 146
Firebelly Design
2701 W Thomas, 2nd Floor
Chicago, IL 60622
USA
T. 773.489.3200
F. 773.489.3439
info@firebellydesign.com

049, 052
Flore Van Ryn
7 Rue de la Seconde Reine
1180 Bruxelles
Belgium
T. 0477.77.25.22
F. 02.375.44.90
florevanryn@skynet.be

027
Format Design
Grosse Brunnenstr. 63a
22763 Hamburg
Germany
T. 171.177.2127
ettling@formatdesign.net

010, 047
Frost Design, Sydney
Level 1, 15 Foster Street
Surry Hills 2010, Sydney
Australia
T. 2.9280.4233
F. 2.9280.4266
diana.czechowska@
frostdesign.com.au

132, 133
Gollings & Pidgeon
147 Chapel Street
St. Kilda, Victoria
Australia
T. 3.9537.0733
F. 3.9537.0187
david.pidgeon@
gollingspidgeon.com

104, 107
HGV
2-6 Northburgh Street
London EC1V 0AY
UK
T. 0207.336.6336
F. 0207.336.6345
pierre@hgv.co.uk

050
Hartford Design
954 W. Washington, 4th Floor
Chicago, IL 60607
USA
T. 312.563.5600
F. 312.563.5603
tim@hartforddesign.com

006, 026, 046, 162, 169
Hat-Trick Design
3 Morocco Street, 3rd Floor
London SE1 3HB
UK
T. 020.7403.7875
F. 020.7403.8926
rachael@hat-trickdesign.
co.uk

172
HvAD
45 Main Street, #1210
Brooklyn, NY 11201
USA
T. 646.345.8455
F. 718.624.3232
henk@hvadesign.com

080
IAAH
727 Duffosat Street
New Orleans, LA 70115
USA
T. 205.401.8001
ness@iamalwayshungry.com

029, 078, 083, 088
Ico Design Consultancy
75-77 Great Portland Street
London W1W 7CR
UK
T. 020.7323.1088
F. 020.7323.1245
sam.nettleton@icodesign.
co.uk

043, 170
Inaria
10 Plato Place 72-74 Street,
Dionis Road, Parsons
Green
London SW6 4TU
UK
T. 020.7384.0900
F. 020.7751.0305
georgie@inaria-design.com

014
**Iridium, a Design
Agency/Kolegram**
43 Eccles Street, 2nd Floor
Ottawa, Ontario KIR 6S3
Canada
T. 613.748.3336
F. 613.748.3372
jeanluc@iridium192.com

095, 096
Kamper Brands
510 Washington Avenue,
South
Minneapolis, MN 55415
USA
T. 612.362.0000
F. 612.238.3851
sanderson@kamperbrands.
com

032
Karakter Ltd
14–18 Old Street
London EC1V 9BH
UK
T. 020.7553.9020
F. 020.7253.9020
crohald@karakter.co.uk

131, 177
Kerr/Noble
Studio 53,
Pennybank Chambers
33–35 St. John's Square
London EC1M 4DS
UK
T. 020.7608.1024
frith@kerrnoble.com

069
Kinetic Singapore
2 Leng Kee Road
Thye Hong Centre #04-03A
Singapore 159086
Singapore
T. 63795792
F. 64725440
roy@kinetic.com.sg

175
Kolegram
37 St. Joseph Boulevard
Gatineau Quebec
Canada
T. 819.777.5538
F. 819.777.8525
gblais@kolegram.com

036, 094, 143, 144, 145
LSD
San Andrés, 36 2o P6
Madrid 28004
Spain
T. 915.943.813
gabriel@lsdspace.com

012, 044, 122, 156
Lippa Pearce
358A Richmond Road
Twickenham TW1 2DU
UK
T. 0208.744.2100
F. 0208.744.2770
abigail@lippapearce.com

042
**Michal Granit Design
Studio**
PO Box 303
Sdeh Varburg, 44935
Israel
T. 9.7469243
F. 9.7446493
granit@zahav.net.il

112
**Mike Lackersteen
Design**
35 Rochester Square
London NW1 9RZ
UK
T. 020.7485.1496
mlackersteen@twindesk.
com

056
Miriello Grafico Inc.
419 West 6 Street
San Diego, CA 92101
USA
T. 619.234.1124
F. 619.234.1960
dennis@miriellografico.
com

064
Murphy Design
1240 Golden Gate Drive
San Diego, CA 92116
USA
T. 619-743-0405
murphy@murphydesign.
com

111, 182
Mytton Williams
15 St. James's Parade
Bath BA1 1UL
UK
T. 01225.442634
F. 01225.442639
design@myttonwilliams.
co.uk

013, 020, 034, 099, 106, 114,
118, 148, 149, 180
NB:Studio
24 Store Street
London WC1E 7BA
UK
T. 020.7580.9195
F. 020.7580.9196
email@nbstudio.co.uk

092
**Nina David
Kommunikationsdesign**
Niederkasseler Kirchweg 56
Duesseldorf 40547
Germany
T. 211.550.86.87
F. 211.550.92.78
mail@ninadavid.de

141
Ó!
Ármúli 11
Reykjavik 108
Iceland
T. 354.562.3300
F. 354.562.3300
einar@oid.is

153
**Pentagram Design,
Berlin**
Leibnizstrasse 60
Berlin 10629
Germany
T. 30.2787610
F. 30.27876110
info@pentagram.de

033, 037, 109, 113, 157
**Pentagram Design,
London**
11 Needham Road
London W11 2RP
UK
T. 020.7229.3477
F. 020.7727.9932
email@pentagram.co.uk

021, 022, 031, 089, 136, 178
**Pentagram Design,
San Francisco**
387 Tehama Street
San Francisco, CA 94103
USA
T. 415.896.0499
F. 415.896.0555
info@sf.pentagram.com

171
Poulin + Morris Inc.
286 Spring Street, 6th Floor
New York, NY 10013
USA
T. 212.675.1332
F. 212.675.3027
info@poulinmorris.com

165
Prime Creative Ltd.
Buckley Farm Studio
Buckley Lane
Halifax HX2 0RQ
UK
T. 01422.340220
F. 01422.348883
peter.rourke@
primecreative.com

137, 176
RB-M
100 De Beauvoir Road
London N1 4EN
UK
T. 020.7923.4040
rbm@mac.com

160
Red Design
Studio 1.1, 11 Jew Street
Brighton BN1 1UT
UK
T. 01273.704614
F. 01273.704615
keith@red-design.co.uk

063
Re-Public
Laplandsgade 4, 1st Floor
Copenhagen 2300 S
Denmark
T. 7020.9890
F. 7020.9690
emil@re-public.com

024, 040, 117
Rose
The Old School, 70 St.
Mary Church Street
London SE16 4HZ
UK
T. 020.7394.2800
F. 020.7394.2980
simon@rosedesign.co.uk

097, 098, 105, 147
Russell Warren-Fisher
Beech House, Bradford Road
Hawthorn, Wiltshire
UK
T. 01225.811.101
russell@rwfhq.com

001, 016, 134, 135
SAS Design
6 Salem Road
London W2 4BU
UK
T. 0207.243.3232
F. 0207.243.3216
abaird@sasdesign.co.uk

167, 179
**Sägenvier Design
Kommunikation**
Sagerstrasse 4
6850 Dornbirn, Vorarlberg
Austria
T. 5572.27481
F. 5572.27484
ramoser@saegenvier.at

002, 051, 054, 123
Sagmeister Inc.
222 West 14 Street
New York, NY 10011
USA
T. 212.647.1789
F. 212.647.1788
stefan@sagmeister.com

003, 023, 030
Salterbaxter
202 Kensington Church
Street
London W8 4DP
UK
T. 020.7229.5720
F. 020.7229.5721
rmcmullan@salterbaxter.com

084, 100, 102, 150
SEA
70 St John Street
London EC1M 4DT
UK
T. 020.7566.3100
F. 020.7566.3101
jondowling@seadesign.co.uk

038, 066
Segura Inc.
1110 North Milwaukee
Avenue
Chicago, IL 60622
USA
T. 773.862.5667
F. 773.862.1214
carlos@segura-inc.com

017
Sonsoles Llorens S.L.
Casp 56 4o D
08010 Barcelona
Spain
T. 934.124.171
F. 934.124.298
info@sonsoles.com

073
stilradar
Schwabstr. 10a
70197 Stuttgart
Germany
T. 711.887.55.20
F. 711.882.23.44
pohland@stilradar.de

174
Stoltze Design
49 Melcher Street, 4th Floor
Boston, MA 02210
USA
T. 617.350.7109
F. 617.482.1171
mary@stoltze.com

101, 108, 110, 151, 183
Studio Myerscough
26 Drysdale Street
London N1 6LS
UK
T. 020.7729.2760
morag@studiomyerscough.
co.uk

061
Subplot Design Inc.
301-318 Homer Street
Vancouver BC V6B 2VZ
Canada
T. 604.685.2990
F. 604.685.2909
roy@subplot.com

071, 072
Taxi Studio Ltd.
93 Princess Victoria Street
Clifton, Bristol BS8 4DD
UK
T. 01179.735151
F. 01179.735181
lydia@taxistudio.co.uk

048, 053
There
Level 1, 16 Foster Street,
Surry Hills
Sydney 2010
Australia
T. 612.9280.1477
F. 612.9280.1499
jackie@there.com.au

164
Timespin
Sophienstrasse 1
Jena, D-07743
Germany
T. 3641.35970
F. 3641.359711
t.schmidt@timespin.de

058, 163
Together Design
106 Cleveland Street
London W1T 6NX
UK
T. 020.7387.7755
F. 020.7387.8555
katja@togetherdesign.co.uk

120
Tomato Košir S.P.
Britof 141
Kranj, Slovenia, SI-4000
Slovenia, EU
T. 386.41.260.979
tomato@tomatokosir.com

059
Turnstyle
2219 New Market Street
Seattle, WA 98107
USA
T. 206.297.7350
F. 206.297.7390
steve@turnstylestudio.com

173
unfolded
Weststrasse 95
Zurich, 8003
Switzerland
T. 44.450.25.82
F. 44.461.05.86
we@unfolded.ch

060, 127
**Viva Dolan Communica-
tions & Design Inc.**
99 Crown's Lane, Suite 500
Toronto, Ontario M5R 3P4
Canada
T. 416.923.6355
F. 416.923.8136
frank@vivadolan.com

155
Voice
217 Gilbert Street
Adelaide, South Australia
5000
Australia
T. 618.8410.8822
F. 618.8410.8933
anthony@voicedesign.net

152, 181
Why Not Associates
22c Shepherdess Walk
London N1 7LB
UK
T. 020.7253.2244
F. 020.7253.2299
andy@whynotassociates.
com

ILLUSTRATION	PHOTOGRAPHY	TYPE ONLY	FOUND ART	STOCK	RECYCLED
TEXTURED	COLORED	COATED	UNCOATED	VELLUM	BOARD
4 COLOR	DIGITAL	2 COLOR	XEROGRAPHY	DUOTONE	TRITONE
QUADRATONE	SPECIALS	SCREENPRINT	LETTERPRESS	ENGRAVING	THERMOGRA-PHY
FOIL-STAMPING	EMBOSSING	DIE-CUT	LAMINATE	PERFECT BOUND	WIRE-O
FRENCH FOLD	HAND-STITCHED	CASE BOUND	SIDE-STITCHED	SADDLE-STITCHED	ACCORDIAN
BINDING POST	GATE FOLD	SERIF	SANS SERIF	HAND DRAWN	GROTESQUE